LATIN HISTORICAL
INSCRIPTIONS

LATIN HISTORICAL INSCRIPTIONS
ILLUSTRATING THE HISTORY
OF THE EARLY EMPIRE
BY G. McN. RUSHFORTH

SECOND EDITION

BOOKS FOR LIBRARIES PRESS
FREEPORT, NEW YORK

First Published 1893
Second Edition 1930
Reprinted 1970

STANDARD BOOK NUMBER:
8369-5196-4

LIBRARY OF CONGRESS CATALOG CARD NUMBER:
70-107831

PRINTED IN THE UNITED STATES OF AMERICA

PREFACE

—*—

THIS collection of inscriptions, arranged on the plan
of Mr. Hicks' well-known *Manual of Greek Historical
Inscriptions*—between which work and my own I must
deprecate any further comparison — is intended to serve
two purposes. In the first place I hope that it may
provide an elementary handbook of Epigraphy, and
secondly that it may help to supply historical information about that period of Roman History in which
the ordinary student in Oxford is still, even after the
publication of Mr. Furneaux's edition of the *Annals*, most
in need of assistance. It will be seen at once that the
historical side has been made the most important. Epigraphy in fact has only been introduced so far as it was
necessary to make the inscriptions intelligible for historical
purposes. The object which I have set before myself has
been to enable the younger class of students to realise the
value of inscriptions as historical evidence, a truth about
which they hear so much but which they have so little
opportunity of verifying. It is hardly too much to say
that in presence not merely of the *Corpus* but even of
selections like that of Wilmanns, the ordinary student is
almost helpless. It has been my endeavour to supply
that historical setting which is necessary if an inscription
is to yield all the information which it contains. At the

same time, so far as the material allowed, I have aimed at
including all the most prominent features in the history
and institutions of the Early Empire, and more particularly
at the epoch of its foundation, the reign of Augustus.

The greater part of the inscriptions are taken from the
Corpus and reproduce the text there given with small
modifications, such as the occasional omission of fragmentary lines or letters which would only confuse the
learner and add nothing to the historical information. The
appearance of the inscriptions in the *Corpus* has also been
imitated as far as possible by the use of capitals, but it
must be remembered that the representations are only
approximate and must not be thought of as facsimiles of
the originals. The longer documents have been printed
in ordinary type, the arrangement of the lines in the
original being preserved in order to facilitate reference.
The inscriptions are supplemented by a certain number
of coins. The text is that of Cohen, and the reference
to Eckhel has been added where the coin was described
by him.

There are a number of books such as Mr. Furneaux's
Annals of Tacitus, Smith's *Dictionary of Antiquities* (third
edition), Schiller's *Geschichte der römischen Kaiserzeit*, &c.,
to which I have been constantly referring but which I
have not thought it necessary to cite on every occasion.
I have added a list of the less obvious authorities to which
more than one reference has been made.

Before I conclude I must acknowledge my obligations
to those who have given their time and knowledge towards
making this book more useful and more correct. Those
obligations are particularly great to Professor Pelham,
without whose encouragement and help this collection
would never have appeared. He has taken the keenest

interest in the work in all its stages, and when I say that everything that I have written has had the benefit of his revision it will be understood how much my book owes to him. I am also very greatly indebted to Mr. F. Haver-field of Christ Church, who besides carefully revising the text of the book has suggested many improvements in arrangement and has always been ready to place his knowledge of Roman inscriptions and antiquities at my service. I have also to thank Mr. W. Warde Fowler of Lincoln College for assistance on points connected with Roman religion; Professor Ramsay of Aberdeen for an important piece of information about No. 95 which I have there acknowledged; and Mr. H. Stuart Jones of Trinity College for verifying from the original a doubtful reading in No. 35. Last but not least Mr. J. A. R. Munro of Lincoln College has not only gone through the labour of reading the sheets, but has made not a few suggestions which I think will add to the usefulness of this book.

G. McN. R.

Oxford:
2 *February,* 1893.

PREFACE TO THE SECOND EDITION

This book has been out of print for some years. As a representative selection of historical inscriptions it was always inadequate; and, indeed, its original purpose was largely to provide beginners with information about the Early Empire which at that time (now more than thirty-five years ago) was not so accessible in English as it is to-day. To recast the book in a new and extended form was not found to be practicable, but as it appears to be still found useful for educational purposes, it was decided to reproduce it by photography, with such corrections and improvements

in the text and references as were possible : e. g. most of
the references to Wilmanns' *Exempla* and Cohen's *Médailles
Impériales* have been altered to the corresponding ones in
Dessau's selection and the new catalogue of Roman Imperial Coins in the British Museum.   In one case (No. 69)
where the inscription had been found to belong to a different
period, an entirely new text has been substituted.   I have
also been able to insert some pages of Addenda and
Corrigenda, in which an attempt has been made to correct
erroneous or misleading statements in the text, and to give
information about new facts or views which have been
published in recent years.   For almost the whole of this
new matter I am indebted to Professor J. G. C. Anderson
and Mr. H. M. Last, who may be said to have fathered this
reissue in the same way that the late Professor Pelham
and Mr. (as he then was) Haverfield did its original form ;
but, as before, the share of the Camden Professor has been
the largest.[1]   My gratitude to them, not to be expressed in
words, will I hope be shared by all who find this collection
useful for the purpose with which it was originally compiled
—to make the history of the Early Roman Empire more
intelligible.

G. McN. R.

Malvern :
November 1929.

---

[1] In a few cases their initials are appended to notes for which they are
specially responsible.

INTRODUCTION

—+—

[The following notes only treat of Epigraphy in so far as points requiring explanation occur in the Inscriptions contained in this collection. Forms which do not appear more than once are dealt with in the headings of the particular Inscriptions. The best introduction to the subject is R. Cagnat's *Cours d'Épigraphie Latine*, 4th Edition, Paris, 1914. The best English book is *Latin Epigraphy* by the late Sir J. E. Sandys, 2nd Edition, Cambridge, 1927.

LATIN monumental inscriptions of the best period are invariably composed of ordinary capitals, and therefore present no difficulty so far as the characters are concerned. Attention however is called to the following usages.

Every word in a line ought to be separated from those which precede and follow it by a stop (*punctum*) placed at the height of the middle of the letters. **Stops.** Abnormally stops occur at the beginning or end of a line (Nos. 11, 68), and even between the syllables of a word or the parts of a numeral (No. 8. 5). Their use or omission is often arbitrary. The *puncta* are sometimes replaced by ivy leaves, e. g. Nos. 12, 60.

The letters in different lines of an inscription may be of different sizes, the most important words or names being larger than the rest (Nos. 8, 10, &c.), **Letters.** but the letters in one line are regularly of the same size. I however often rises above the line. Originally this represented *ei*, but by the time of Augustus its use had become arbitrary, and in some words it is conventional, e. g. ᴅIᴠI (Nos. 1, 3, &c.), and Iᴍᴘ (Nos. 1, 24, &c.). In the latter case it has no analogy with the modern use of capital letters at the beginning of a word or sentence. The upper part of letters which stand upon a single vertical stroke (ᴛ, ʏ) is also sometimes extended above the line so as to economise space (Nos. 56, 61, &c.).

Accents. An accent (*apex*) is often placed over long vowels, but its use is irregular and arbitrary. Nos. 3, 14, &c.

Numerals. Letters used as numerals are often distinguished by a line above them. Abbreviations are occasionally marked in the same way (Nos. 10. 5, 14. 6, 48. 8).

Ligatures. A practice which grew more frequent as time went on was that of joining two (sometimes more) letters, generally by making their vertical strokes coincide. Nos. 18, 67, &c.

Orthography. Under Augustus the long *i* is still occasionally represented by *ei*, especially in the dative and ablative plural (Nos. 2, 29. 3). Cf. also in No. 32. 2: *ceivitatium* ; 4: *ceivitates.*

The genitive and dative singular of the first declension in -*ai* is found as late as Augustus (No. 34. 6), and was one of the archaisms restored by Claudius. No. 86. 4, and cf. *Caisar* in 71. 1, 73. 2.

The single *i* is commoner than *ii* in the dative and ablative plural of nouns in *ia, ius, ium,* of the first and second declension, in the genitive singular of those in *ius, ium,* and in the nominative plural of those in *ius.*

Examples of irregularity in spelling are not infrequent in provincial inscriptions, e. g. No. 99.

The difficulties in reading inscriptions arise either (1) from the fact that many words are abbreviated or represented only by their initial letter; (2) or from the fact that many inscriptions are mutilated and have to be restored.

Owing to the formal character of most inscriptions a large number of abbreviations are fixed and recur regularly. It is simplest therefore to explain them in connection with the formulae in which they are found. A list of all the abbreviations not explained in the text will be found on p. xxxii The expansion of an abbreviation is always enclosed in round brackets. **Abbreviations.**

A Roman name when fully expressed in an inscription contains the following elements. It is not unusual to find some of them omitted. **Names.**

(1) *Praenomen.* Always represented by the initial letter, except CN = *Gnaeus*, SER = *Servius*, SEX = *Sextus*, TI = *Tiberius* (to distinguish it from T = *Titus*).

(2) *Nomen.*

(3) The father's *praenomen*, abbreviated as above, in the genitive followed by *f*(*ilius*). Occasionally further generations are given, e. g. No. 16.

(4) Name of the tribe in the ablative. Nearly always represented by its first three letters.

(5) *Cognomen.*

(6) Sometimes the domicile or place of origin is added in the ablative, especially in the case of soldiers. E.g. No. 77. 2.

In the names of freedmen (3) is replaced by the *praenomen* (sometimes the full name) of the previous owner in the genitive followed by *l*(*ibertus*). A freedman of an Emperor is described as *Aug*(*usti*) *l*(*ibertus*). No. 75. For the formula in cases where the owner was a woman see No. 45.

Slaves are described by a single name followed by the owner's *praenomen* or full name in the genitive with or without *s*(*ervus*). Nos. 39, 40, &c.

When persons have taken part in public life (including priesthoods) either in the State or in their own municipalities, the different offices which they have held are inscribed after the name in order of dignity, the most important generally coming last (e. g. **Official Titles.**

Nos. 23, 60, 93), but sometimes this order is reversed and the most important come first (e.g. No. 27). The titles are nearly always abbreviated: *co(n)s(ul)*, *pr(aetor)*, *q(uaestor)*, *leg(atus)*. When an office is of the collegiate form the number is generally written with a numeral: IIVIR=*duumvir*, &c. Iteration may be expressed by a numeral following the title (e.g. No. 23. 18).

Emperors' names and titles follow a regular order. With **Emperors.** the Emperors of the first dynasty the form of the name had not become fixed, but that taken by Augustus was the one finally adopted, and it is treated here as normal, the principal exceptions being noted under the various headings. The commonest abbreviations are indicated by brackets.

(1) *Imp(erator)*, the *praenomen Imperatoris* (Suet. Iul. 76). Tiberius (No. 14), Gaius (No. 54), and Claudius (No. 71), never accepted the *praenomen Imperatoris* and consequently each of them uses his own *praenomen*. Sometimes also Vitellius (No. 68).

(2) *Caesar*.

(3) Name of the father in the genitive followed by *f(ilius)*. When the father is a deified Emperor, *divi* is added. In the case of Augustus, when Caesar was the only person who had received *consecratio*, the form is *divi f(ilius)*. The remoter ascendants are sometimes added with *n(epos)*, *pron(epos)*, *abn(epos)*. No. 92.

(4) *Aug(ustus)*.

(5) In the case of Gaius, Claudius, and Nero, the name *Germanicus* follows. It is derived from their common ancestor the elder Drusus, who had the title conferred on him. Later Emperors insert in the same place names derived from victories (*Dacicus*, *Parthicus*, &c.). The use of *Germanicus* by Vitellius is the earliest trace of this practice (p. 80).

(6) *Pontifex Maximus*, abbreviated in various ways.

(7) *Trib(unicia) Potest(ate)*, *Tribuniciae Potestatis*, followed by the numeral giving the year of the tenure.

N. B.—The tribunician year does not coincide with the actual year, but is reckoned from the day on which the power was conferred—in the case of Augustus, e. g., June 26 or 27 (St. R. ii. 797, note 3)—or in the case of the successors of Augustus from the *dies imperii* (St. R. ii. 796–798). Tables of the tribunician years of all the Emperors will be found in Cagnat, p. 177 sqq.

(8) *Imp(erator)* followed by a numeral, the *acclamatio imperatoria* assumed after military successes gained by the Emperor or under his auspices. The first military success was expressed by IMP II, and so on, IMP I being assumed at accession.

(9) *Co(n)s(ul)* followed by a numeral to express the number of times held, and in case the Emperor has been elected for the next year, by *design(atus)*. With Augustus the consulship comes before (7).

(10) *P(ater) P(atriae)*.

It will be noticed that (7) (8) (9) determine the date of the inscription.

FORM OF INSCRIPTIONS.

The inscriptions contained in this selection, which are fairly representative of monumental inscriptions generally, may be classed under the following heads.

Inscriptions proper (*tituli*), the essence of which is the name of an individual and a statement of his relation to the monument on which it is inscribed, must be distinguished from the various kinds of public acts or documents (the most general name for which is *acta*) engraved upon stone or metal.

I. Inscriptions Proper.

Epitaphs. Epitaphs take various forms, and the following classification cannot be regarded as fixed. Ordinarily, however, epitaphs contain two parts—

(*a*) The name of the deceased accompanied by his official description or career, either—

    (1) In the nominative, followed by *h*(*ic*) *s*(*itus*) *e*(*st*) or some equivalent. E. g. Nos. 18, 99.

    (2) Or in the genitive, depending on *D*(*is*) *M*(*anibus*), which is also sometimes prefixed independently to the other forms. No. 11.

    (3) Or in the dative. No. 10.

(*b*) The name of the person who has erected the memorial, in the nominative. Nos. 10, 18, &c.

N.B.—(i) Statements of age (generally expressed by *ann*(*orum*) followed by a numeral) are not usual in the case of persons whose official career is given. With soldiers *stip*(*endiorum*) is added. No. 67.

(ii) Sometimes a formula is added protecting the tomb. No. 23. 22.

(iii) No. 23, in which the deceased speaks in the first person, is abnormal. The more elaborate *elogia* sometimes found on tombs are illustrated by No. 93. Nos. 54 and 55 are not to be classed as epitaphs. The epitaphs would occupy a conspicuous position on the outer face of the Augustan Mausoleum.

Honorary Inscriptions. Honorary inscriptions are generally inscribed on the pedestal of a statue erected to an individual in his lifetime. The commonest type gives the name of the person with his titles and offices in the dative, followed by that of the community or person who has erected it in the nominative, concluding with some expression which indicates the occasion or reason of the erection. Nos. 17, 37, 76, 100, are typical.

Votive inscriptions are those which are connected with an image, altar, or temple of a divinity. The regular type has the name of the divinity in the dative, *sacrum* being sometimes added, and that of the dedicator in the nominative. At the end there is generally some formula which expresses the act of offering: *d(edit) d(edicavit)*, *v(otum) s(olvit)*, &c. Nos. 46, 48, 61, 83–85, are typical. The authorisation of the municipal senate is often added in the form *ex d(ecreto) d(ecurionum)*. Nos. 40, 43.

Votive Inscriptions.

The inscriptions which belong to public works and monuments generally explain themselves and contain no peculiarities. E. g. Nos. 24, 71, 72, 74, 81.

Inscriptions connected with Public Works.

With these are to be classed the inscriptions on the series of *cippi* and columns connected with roads and boundaries.

Milestones (*miliaria*) give the name of the Emperor, in the first century usually in the nominative, followed in the case of Imperial roads in the provinces by the name of the *legatus* and of the legion which made the road, the two latter generally in the ablative. The name of the place from which the road starts (*caput viae*) is generally added, and the number of miles from this point is given at the end. Nos. 8, 9, 22, 33, 98.

Milestones.

The *cippi terminales* used for defining public land, the course of the Tiber, the line of the Pomerium, &c., are inscribed on similar principles. Their peculiar forms are explained in the instances given. Nos. 25, 26, 73.

Boundary Stones.

The large class of inscriptions (containing little beyond the name of the maker or producer) found upon pottery, bricks, marble in block, pigs of lead, &c., is represented in this selection only by a reference, Addenda p. xxvii. These were made in the army for use in military works, and are stamped with the name of the legion, or, in the case of a composite force, with the names of all the legions which make it up.

II. Documents.

To be distinguished from inscriptions proper are documents the original and appropriate form for which is Manuscript, but which for purposes of publication are engraved on marble, stone, or bronze. Those which occur here may be classed as follows.

For the double character of No. 70 as a *lex* and a *senatus consultum* see p. 84, and cf. the form of No. 35.

Laws. The Imperial Edicts (Nos. 79, 82) belong to the category of *leges* (see Ulpian, quoted on p. 86). With them may be classed the grants of citizenship to soldiers on their discharge (*diplomata militaria, privilegia veteranorum*), of which No. 78 is an example. They

Diplomata Militaria. take the form of bronze diptychs professing to contain certified copies of the original grants preserved at Rome (No. 78. 19). The original contained the names of all the soldiers who were discharged at the same time (cf. l. 7 : *quorum nomina subscripta sunt*), but the copy only gives the name of the individual for whose benefit it was made (l. 18). Hence some examples give a reference to the place in the original document where the name occurred (e. g. *C. I. L.* iii. p. 846, l. 5 : *pag. II. kap. XVI*, and cf. pp. 847, 848, which are two copies from the same grant). The grant is inscribed on the inner side of one of the leaves of the diptych, and the names and seals of the seven witnesses who attested the copy on the other. The grant alone is repeated on the outer sides. For descriptions of the diptychs see Mommsen in *C. I. L.* iii. p. 902 ; Sandys, *Latin Epigraphy*, p. 180 ; Cagnat, *Cours d'Épigraphie*, p. 302.

Among the sacerdotal colleges the Arval Brotherhood is

Acta of Religious Corporations. the only one the *Acta* of which have come down to us in any appreciable quantity. No. 66. The fragments, extending from the time of Augustus to the middle of the third century, contain, in addition to the account of the three-days festival of the Dea

Dia (on the second of which the famous *carmen* was sung) and notices relating to the appointment of new members of the college, records of various religious observances connected with events in the lives of the reigning Emperor and members of his family, and thus often provide contemporary evidence as to dates. The greater part of the fragments were discovered in the Vigna Ceccarelli about five miles from Rome on the road to Porto, corresponding to the *lucus deae Diae via Campana apud lapidem quintum* mentioned in the *Acta* for Nov. 7, A.D. 224, *C. I. L.* vi. p. 575. See Henzen, *Acta Fratrum Arvalium* (Berlin, 1874). *C.I.L.* vi. p. 459, *Eph. Epigr.* ii. p. 211, viii. p. 316. Typical selections will be found in Dessau's *Inscr. Lat. Sel.* i, p. 58 ; ii, p. 267.

The Roman Calendars (illustrated by No. 4) are arranged in the form of columns each of which contains a different set of notices about the days of the month. **Calendars.**

(1) The first column contains the *littera nundinalis* or day of the week ; the year being divided into weeks of eight days (*nundinae*, the eighth day) marked by the first eight letters of the alphabet. In No. 4, **E.**

(2) The second column gives the day of the month, either one of the fixed points (*Kalendae, Nonae, Idus* in No. 4 represented by **EID**) or the number of the day before the next fixed point.

(3) The third column indicates the character of the day, e. g. whether *fastus* (**F**), *comitialis* (**C**), *nefastus* (**N**); a *dies nefastus hilarior* being distinguished by the archaic form of **N**, as in No. 4.

(4) Lastly come various notices about the day, religious observances connected with it, or events commemorated on it; and, when these occur for the first time, explanations of the name of the day (*Kalendae*, &c.). In No. 4 the explanation of *Idus* is too fragmentary to be restored.

No. 38 is an example of a *Feriale* or Calendar of a particular

b

local cult outside Rome. As only the feast-days are mentioned, the entries are confined to the date, the event commemorated, and the religious observance connected with it.

The fragments of the various Calendars which have been
discovered in Rome and Italy are collected in *C.I.L.* i. p. 293
sqq., vi. p. 625 sqq.; Dessau, ii. pp. 250, 987.

The lists of magistrates arranged in chronological order, of

Fasti. which the *Fasti Consulares* are the most important, are represented here only by the extract
from the *Fasti Feriarum Latinarum*, No. 5. They contain
only the date of the festival and the names of the Consuls
of the year who officiated. See *C.I.L.* vi. p. 455, xiv. p. 213 ;
Eph. Epigr. ii. p. 93.

The Ancyran Monument is only made use of in the present
The Monu- volume for purposes of illustration like the
mentum literary sources, but it is quoted and referred to
Ancyranum. so often in Part I that it may be well to give a
short account of it.

The *Res gestae divi Augusti quibus orbem terrarum imperio
populi Romani subiecit et impensae quas in rem publicam popu-
lumque Romanum fecit*—to quote the heading of the document—are inscribed on the inside walls of the Pronaos of the
Temple of Augustus and Roma at Ancyra in Galatia. The
heading further informs us that what follows is a copy of an
original engraved *in duabus aheneis pilis quae sunt Romae
positae.* It is clear then that Suetonius is referring to the
same original when he mentions the *indicem rerum a se ges-
tarum quem incidi vellet* (*Augustus*) *in aeneis tabulis quae ante
Mausoleum statuerentur* (Aug. 101, cf. Dio Cass. 56. 33). It
was apparently reproduced at Ancyra by way of doing honour
to the memory of Augustus, and as was natural in the Greek-
speaking part of the Empire, a Greek translation was engraved
on one of the outer walls of the temple. The contents of the
document are sufficiently indicated by the heading quoted
above, and it is not possible to class it under any particular

kind of inscriptions. The view that it is an epitaph is forced, but Mommsen has pointed out that the nearest analogy is to be found in the inscription of the tomb of Antiochus of Commagene on the Nimrud Dagh near the Euphrates (*Historische Zeitschrift*, 1887, 385. Cf. Mommsen, *Provinces*, ii. 125).

For the principles on which mutilated or fragmentary inscriptions can be restored see Cagnat, *Cours*, 379. Here it will be enough to point out that in many cases the restoration is determined by— **Restorations.**

(1) The ascertained limits of the inscription. The length of the lines and the size of the letters being known, the number of letters required can be fixed. E. g. No. 86.

(2) The formal character of inscriptions. If certain data are preserved the rest can be supplied with certainty. E. g. the names and titles of Emperors (e. g. No. 29). So in documents which contain many legal formulae: e. g. No. 35.

Restorations are added in italics where the inscription itself is reproduced, and within square brackets where the inscription is expanded.

COINS.

As coins only take a subordinate place in this selection, it will not be necessary here to notice more than the following elementary facts about them. For further information see Cohen, *Médailles Imp.* i, Introduction p. xiii. Hirschfeld, *Verwaltungsbeamten*, 92.

Under the Empire the coinage of gold and silver belongs to the Emperor, that of bronze to the Senate.

The gold coins are the denarius, known as the *aureus* (= 25 silver denarii), and its half the *quinarius*.

The silver coins are the *denarius* and *quinarius*.

The bronze coins are conventionally described as—

>   Large bronze
>   Middle   „
>   Small   „

The head of the Emperor appears on these just as on the Imperial coins, but the reverse is marked with *S(enatus) C(onsulto)*.

CORRIGENDA AND ADDENDA

p. xviii. *Monumentum Ancyranum.*

On the site of Antioch in Pisidia (see under No. 22) Sir W. M. Ramsay discovered in 1914 and 1924 fragments of another copy of the *Res Gestae Divi Augusti* (without the Greek version). Some of the corrections are of importance. It has been edited by W. M. Ramsay and A. von Premerstein as the *Monumentum Antiochenum* in *Klio*, Beiheft xix (Leipzig, 1927). See also Ramsay in *J. R. S.* vi (1916), 108 ff.

p. xix. *Coins.*

For the Imperial coinage see now H. Mattingly's *Coins of the Roman Empire in the British Museum*, vol. i, Augustus to Vitellius (London, 1923), esp. pp. xliv ff.

The bronze or token coins are now described as the

Sestertius = 4 asses
Dupondius = 2 asses } struck in orichalcum,

As
Quadrans or quarter of the As } struck in copper.

pp. 4–8. *Constitution of the Principate.*

Pelham's theory (on which the statements of pp. 5–7 were based) that the imperium of Augustus was essentially consular, though described as proconsular when applied to the provinces, has not stood the test of criticism, and E. G. Hardy's statement of the case (*Studies in Roman History*, i. 284 ff.) should be substituted. In the last century of the Republic the consulate had been practically confined to urban or home duties, and the provincial proconsulate had become a distinct magistracy. Under the Principate these became fixed rules, nor was there any exception in the case of the Emperor. Augustus held the consulship for purposes of home government only (including the Census), but after B.C. 23 only twice (B.C. 5 and 2), so that the loss of rights connected with home administration involved in its abandonment had to be gradually made good in various ways, some of which elude certain explanation. For his control of provincial administration he depended on an extended *proconsulare imperium* which he was empowered to exercise from (not over) Rome. Dio Cassius, liii. 32. 5 (quoted on p. 7).

pp. 9-11. *Spain.*

No. 7 (which the title *pater patriae* dates as in or after B. C. 2) does not refer to the general pacification of Spain, but probably expresses the gratitude of the province of Baetica for the rearrangement of the boundary between it and Hispania Citerior (or Tarraconensis), carried out before B.C. 2 as shown by No. 9, by which the region of the Saltus Castulonensis (Sierra Morena) with its secular traditions of brigandage (cf. Cicero, *Epp. ad Fam.* x. 31. 1) was transferred to the latter, where there were troops that could deal with it, the boundary being thenceforward the Baetis.

E. Albertini, *Les divisions administratives de l'Espagne romaine* (Paris, 1923), pp. 25-41.

p. 10. The force of three legions was maintained only to the reign of Claudius, when the IV Macedonica was sent to the Rhine to replace the XIV Gemina which took part in the invasion of Britain in A. D. 43. Compare No. 67 and *D.* 2283. Ritterling, *Legio*, 1551.

p. 14. *Gallia Narbonensis.*

' Geographical conditions help to explain the history of the three centres of the Vocontii. Lucus Augusti (Luc-en-Diois), on the road which led from the Cottian Alps to Valence, evidently received the Roman *civitas* early, to judge by the number of legionaries who came from it (see *C. I. L.* xii, p. 161 for instances); but its prosperity seems to have been short-lived, and little or no trace of its existence remains (*C. I. L.* xii, p. 161). Dea Augusta (Die), in the same region, had no importance beyond remaining the religious centre of the tribe (for the cult of *dea Andarta* see *C. I. L.* xii. 1554). Vasio (Vaison), on the other hand, lying in a fertile part of the canton, on the edge of the Rhone valley, developed rapidly into a Romanized agricultural town, with all the usual equipment of forum, theatre, baths, &c.; and its predominant position is shown by the facts that all the cantonal officials lived there, and that it was placed on a level with the *pagi* in respect of government (under a *praefectus*, *C. I. L.* xii. 1375; and cf. p. 162).' [J. G. C. A.]

p. 15 note. Hirschfeld, *Gallische Studien*, now in his *Kleine Schriften* (Berlin, 1913), 47 ff. (esp. 83 ff.).

pp. 16, 17. *The Three Gauls.*

Vol. xiii. of the *Corpus*, covering the Three Gauls and Germany, is in course of publication (1899-1907), and Nos. 15, 16, 17 appear in it as 1577, 1036, and 1541 respectively. The inscription referred to at the bottom of p. 17 is now 1684.

The colony mentioned in No. 15 is not Lugudunum but Anicium Vellavorum (Le Puy-en-Velay), which probably received the title from Claudius, thereby gaining a predominant position in the canton, of which, however, it still formed a part. The IIvir (l. 3) is probably the chief magistrate of the canton. Cf. e. g. for the Sequani *C. I. L.* xiii. 1674-5 = *D.* 7013, 4537, dedications by Q. Adginnius Martinus, Seq(uanus), IIvir in civitate Sequanorum.

p. 18. *Gutuater.* See J. Loth in *Revue archéologique*, 5 S. xx (1924), 59 and n. 3.

p. 19. *Pannonian Legions.*

In addition to the evidence for the Eighth Legion at Poetovio (*C. I. L.* iii. 4060, 10878, 10879), it is now believed that the Ninth was probably stationed at Siscia (Sziszek) on the Save, and, after temporary service in Africa against Tacfarinas in A.D. 20 (Tac. *Ann.* iii. 9, iv. 5 and 23), no doubt returned there and remained till the British expedition of A.D. 43 was being formed (Tac. *Ann.* xiv. 32). The Fifteenth was probably quartered near Emona (Laibach) till the end of the reign of Augustus, but later was stationed at Carnuntum, perhaps in connexion with Maroboduus and the German threat to the northern frontier in A.D. 17–18 (Tac. *Ann.* ii. 44 seqq., 62 seqq.).

Ritterling, *Legio*, 1645, 1665, 1747. For Carnuntum see W. Kubitschek & S. Frankfurter, *Führer durch Carnuntum* (Vienna, Oest. Arch. Inst., 1923).

p. 22. *Colonies of Augustus in Pisidia.*

No. 22, l. 5. The name of the road, illegible on the Comama milestone, was proved by another, found by Professor Anderson in 1900 at Yonuslar (*C. I. L.* iii. 14401 *c = D.* 5828), to have been *Via Sebaste* (=Augusta, the imperial road). The name of the *legatus* is given as *Cornuto Aquila*, i.e. Cornutus Arruntius Aquila, governor of Galatia in B.C. 6.

Sir W. M. Ramsay in *J. R. S.* vi (1916), 87, 96.

p. 25. *The Governorships of P. Sulpicius Quirinius.*

The governorships of P. Sulpicius Quirinius have been discussed afresh in connexion with two inscriptions from Antioch in Pisidia in honour of C. Caristanius Fronto Caesianus Julius, who is described as *praefectus* or deputy of P. Sulpicius Quirinius when the latter was honorary *IIvir* of the colony (*D.* 9502, 9503). Strabo (xii, p. 566) says, without giving a date (Tacitus, *Ann.* iii. 48, says that it was before his mission with C. Caesar : see below), that Quirinius subdued the Homonadenses who had killed Amyntas, king of Galatia, about B.C. 25 (when Galatia became a province) ; and it has been supposed that this took place at some time when Quirinius was governor of Syria and Cilicia, presumably about B.C. 11–9, and that the honour conferred on him by Antioch was an expression of its gratitude for the suppression of such dangerous neighbours (G. L. Cheesman in *J. R. S.* iii (1913), 253 ff.; E. Bleckmann in *Klio*, xvii (1921), 104 ff.). Dessau, however, thought that the honour of the duumvirate (very unusual except for members of the Imperial family) was more likely connected with Quirinius's mission in the East as adviser of C. Caesar in A.D. 1–4 (*Klio*, ibid. 252). Hitherto a confirmation of two governorships of Syria by Quirinius was supposed to exist in a fragment of an inscription from Tibur (*C. I. L.* xiv. 3613 = *D.* 918) which reads as follows:

r]egem, qua redacta in pot[estatem imp. Caesaris]
Augusti populique Romani senatu[s dis immortalibus]

supplicationes binas ob res prosp[ere gestas, et]
ipsi ornamenta triumph[alia decrevit] ;
pro consul(e) Asiam provinciam op[tinuit ; legatus pr. pr.]
divi Augusti iterum Syriam et Ph[oenicen optinuit].

Mommsen (*Res Gestae D. Aug.* 161 ff.) assumed that the subject of the epitaph was Quirinius, and that *regem* referred to Amyntas. Recently E. Groag has pointed out (*Jahreshefte des Oesterreich. Arch. Inst.* xxi–xxii (1922–24), Beiblatt, 445) that while the province of a *legatus* of Syria who subdued the Homonadenses must have included Cilicia, the inscription mentions Phoenicia and not Cilicia as united to Syria. For this and other reasons he rejects the identification with Quirinius, and claims the epitaph for M. Plautius Silvanus, consul in B.C. 2 (cf. Nos. 41, 47), and as coming probably from the family mausoleum near Tibur (see No. 93). Plautius's governorship of Syria may have immediately preceded that of Saturninus (A.D. 4–5), or that of Quirinius (A.D. 6). He was summoned from the East to take part in the suppression of the great Pannonian revolt of A.D. 7–9 ; and *regem* of the fragment may refer to Bato, king of the Breuci, against whom he conducted a successful campaign (Dio Cass. lv. 34. 4 ; cf. Vell. Pat. ii. 112. 4). *Iterum* only means that it was a second governorship, that of Asia being the first ; not a second tenure of the same province, which was contrary to the practice of Augustus.

The supposed first Syrian governorship of Quirinius has thus lost the support of the Caristanius and Tibur inscriptions, and has become very doubtful.

p. 29. *The Tiber.*

For more recent information about the *terminatio ripae* see S. B. Platner and T. Ashby, *A Topographical Dictionary of Ancient Rome* (Oxford and London, 1929), p. 537.

p. 30 (3). The full title of the *curatores* was *curatores aedium sacrarum et operum locorumque publicorum populi Romani* (e.g. *D.* 8971), but it was commonly abbreviated in various ways. See Index to Dessau (iii, pt. 1, pp. 357, 8), where some of the instances suggest that in practice one curator dealt with *aedes sacrae* and the other with *opera publica*, the individual being described, if not by the comprehensive title, as curator of the department with which he was specially concerned. [H. M. L.]

As the *curatores* are not mentioned in the Senatus consultum of B.C. 11 (Frontinus, *de Aq.* 100), they must have been instituted after that year. There is no reason to think that the curatorship of Q. Varius Geminus (No. 27) fell as late as the reign of Tiberius. The office was held after either the praetorship or the consulship, but Geminus had not attained to the latter, and after his praetorship he was a proconsul and twice legatus under Augustus. The office would naturally follow his praetorship, and therefore be in the time of Augustus.

p. 31. The board of two *praefecti frumenti dandi*, set up in B.C. 22, and enlarged to four in B.C. 18, was chosen from senators of praetorian rank

(Dio Cass. liv. 1 and 17). The later *praefecti ex senatus consulto* were only exceptionally of inferior standing (mostly ex-praetors), and it is probable that they dealt, not with exceptional distributions, but with the regular *frumentationes*. Hirschfeld, *Verwaltungsbeamten*, 232-237; Cardinali, in Ruggiero's *Dizionario Epigrafico*, iii. 248.

The difference of title in the Sc. of B.C. 11 (Frontinus, loc. cit.) ought to indicate difference of function. We must distinguish between supply and distribution. We may suppose that the original *praefecti* of B.C. 22 dealt with both ; that from B.C. 11 the *curatores* had charge of supply, and the *praefecti* of distribution ; and that finally the *praefectus annonae* controlled supply, and the *praefecti frumenti dandi* distribution. [H.M.L.]

pp. 37–40. *The Alpine Tribes.*

Probably all the Alpine districts were at first placed under *praefecti*. For Raetia see *C.I.L.* ix. 3044=*D.* 2689 : [*S*]*ex. Pedio Sex. f. An*(*iensi*) (*tribu*) *Lusiano Hirruto prim*(*o*)*pil*(*o*) *leg. XXI pra*[*ef*(*ecto*)] *Raetis Vindolicis valli*[*s P*]*oeninae et levis armatur*(*ae*), &c. Noricum may have been governed in the same way (Hirschfeld, *Verwaltungsbeamten*, 383).

p. 44. No. 35. *Provincial Worship of the Emperor.*

Krascheninnikoff has maintained that the Emperor referred to (e. g. l. 13) is Vespasian, not Augustus ; but it is possible that the Imperial cult had been authorized, though not regulated, before the end of Nero's reign. In the time of Augustus institutions of this kind were confined to less civilized regions or ethnical groups, where they were used as instruments of Romanization. For a provincial cult in Lusitania cf. *C. I. L.* ii. 473 = *D.* 6892 (from Mérida) : *Divo Augusto Albinus Albini f. flamen divi Aug. provinciae Lusitaniae.*

M. Krascheninnikoff in *Philologus* liii (1894), 165 ff. E. Kornemann in *Klio* i (1901), 102 ff.

p. 46. No. 37. *Sacerdos Romae et Augusti* is his title as priest of the Imperial cult established by Augustus in the *Conventus Asturum* (cf. *D.* 6932). The Imperial cult of the province of Hither Spain, post-Augustan in origin (Tac. *Ann.* i. 78), was that of the Emperor alone, not of Rome and Augustus, and the priest was a *flamen* (not *sacerdos* as in Augustan foundations) after the pattern of the *flamen Augustalis* of the cult of the Divus Augustus at Rome. The instances are collected in *C. I. L.* ii, pp. 563 ff.

p. 51, note. Hirschfeld's article on the Worship of the Emperor has been reprinted in his *Kleine Schriften*, 471 ff.

p 52. No. 38, l. 10. [XV]III K. Febr. is a mistake for XVII (Jan. 16). See *C. I. L.* i (2nd ed.), p. 307. The date is given correctly in the *Fasti Praenestini* of M. Verrius Flaccus, the contemporary of Augustus (ibid., p. 231).

p. 54. No. 39. Line 4 should read: *minist*]*ri Merc*(*urio*) *Mai*(*ae*) [*s*]*acr*(*um*). *Minister* appears alone in the earliest of these Pompeian dedications (*C. I. L.* x. 884 = *D.* 6388), of B.C. 25. Cf. also *C. I. L.* x. 886 = *D.* 6389 (B.C. 14): *M. Sittius M. l*(*ibertus*) *Serapa Merc*(*urio*) *Maiae sacrum ex d. d.*, &c.

p. 55. No. 43. The date may be later than B.C. 2, as the duumvirate of M. Holconius Rufus is only a *terminus post quem.*

pp. 56–58. *Worship of the Emperor in Italy.*

Prof. L. R. Taylor maintains that a more or less official cult of the living Emperor was probably established by Augustus in every town of Italy; and she gives a list of some sixty places where there is evidence of a *flamen* (rarely *sacerdos*) *Augusti*, or occasionally *Romae et Augusti*, but believes that the worship was not of the Emperor himself, but of his Genius. Nor was it confined to Augustus. For Claudius see *C. I. L.* x. 1558 (Puteoli, A.D. 46), *sacerdoti di*[*vini nostri im*]*peratoris Ti. Claud*[*i Drusi f. Caes. Aug*]*usti Germanici,* &c. Nero even had a *flamen perpetuus* before his accession (*D.* 5145).

Prof. L. R. Taylor, 'The Worship of Augustus in Italy during his lifetime'. *Transactions of the American Philological Association,* li (1920), 116–133.

p. 64. *The Augustales.*

Prof. L. R. Taylor (*J. R. S.* xiv (1924), 158 ff.) would explain the origin of the *Seviri Augustales* by the analogy of the *severi equitum,* officers connected with the games and celebrations of the *equites* at Rome (see Dessau, Indices, iii, pt. 1, p. 410).

p. 66 (bibliography). The reference to Hirschfeld is now *Kleine Schriften,* 508 ff.

p. 75. *L. Verginius Rufus.*

L. Verginius Rufus should be described as a strict constitutionalist rather than a sincere republican. His refusal to accept the Empire offered to him by his army was based on the doctrine that only the old constituent powers, the Senate and Roman People, could confer the *imperium.* See Ph. Fabia, *Klio,* pp. 49 ff.; and cp. O. Th. Schulz, *Das Wesen des römischen Kaisertums der ersten zwei Jahrhunderte,* ch. iii (Bonn, 1916).

pp. 76–78. Nos. 62–65. L. Clodius Macer.

For Macer and his coinage generally see H. Mattingly, *Coins of the Roman Empire in the British Museum,* vol. i, pp. clxxxvi sqq., 285 sqq.; and for No. 63 cp. p. 287 note *, for No. 64 p. 286 note *, and for No. 65, p. 286 note †.

p. 84. *The Lex de Imperio.*

It must be remembered that though the jurists, when explaining what gives validity to the Emperor's *constitutiones,* use *imperium* for the Emperor's powers as a whole, the *imperium* was conferred by the Senate, and the *tribunicia potestas* by a *lex* preceded by a decree of the Senate.

p. 89. No. 73. *The Pomerium.*

The most recent information about the Pomerium will be found in Platner and Ashby's *Topographical Dictionary of Ancient Rome*, 392–396.

p. 92. *Ostia.* 'Undated coins of Nero.'

As the undated sestertii of Nero with representation of the harbour of Ostia (*B. M. C. Emp.* i, pp. 221 ff., nos. 131–135; p. 264, no. 323; cp. p. clxxvi) belong to the later period of his coinage (not before A. D. 64, *op. cit.* p. clxv), Mr. Sydenham has suggested that they refer, not to the completion of the work of Claudius, but to the scheme for a ship-canal from the lake of Avernus to Ostia, one of the projects of Nero's architect-engineers, Severus and Celer, mentioned unsympathetically by Tacitus (*Ann.* xv. 42; cf. Suet. *Nero,* 31; Plin. *N.H.* xiv. 6. 8. 61). Part of it can still be traced on the landward side of Monte Circeio, south of the Pontine Marshes.

E. A. Sydenham, *The Coinage of Nero* (London, Spink, 1920), p. 110.

J. Lugli, *Forma Italiae*, i, pt. 2 (Rome, 1928), pp. xiv. 31, 35; and see Dr. Ashby's review in *J. R. S.* xviii (1928), 110.

p. 94. *Increase of the Urban Cohorts.*

The new urban cohorts were numbered XIV–XVIII. For XIV see *D.* 2081, 2084, &c.; for XV *D.* 2128, 2129, 9199; for XVI *D.* 2648. XVII was stationed at Lugudunum: *D.* 2130, 2131, 9077; cf. Tac. *Ann.* iii. 41. 2 (A.D. 21), and *C. I. L.* xiii, p. 250. By A.D. 69 it was at Ostia (Tac. *Hist.* i. 80), and had been replaced at Lugudunum by XVIII (Tac. *Hist.* i. 64). Vespasian appears to have created a new cohort *I Flavia Urbana*, which took the place of XVIII at Lugudunum not later than A.D. 73: *D.* 2118, 2119.

Though neither No. 76 nor the inscription of L. Coiedius Candidus (p. 95, now *D.* 967) prove that a detachment of the Eighth Legion was sent to Britain, or that the military distinctions mentioned were won there, the fact that there was such a detachment in Britain in A.D. 43 is established by a tile of the legion discovered at Leicester (*Eph. Epigr.* vii. 1124, p. 342; *Archaeological Journal*, lxxv (1918), pp. 25, 26, n. 1; Haverfield and Macdonald, *Roman Occupation of Britain*, 105).

p. 95. No. 77. Introductory note.

Assuming that the years of service are correctly stated in the inscription, if Moderatus lived into the reign of Trajan, the mention of Domitian (*damnatae memoriae*) is very irregular.

pp. 99 ff. No. 79. *Civitas of the Anauni.*

See now E. G. Hardy's edition of the document in his *Roman Laws and Charters* (Oxford, 1912), part ii, 11 ff. The words *mei iuris* (l. 15) do not refer to the Emperor's domain (p. 101, l. 6 from the end), but to the fact that the non-attributed districts were under his control as forming part of the province of Raetia (cf. Hardy, pp. 123, 128 n. 14).

p. 107, last paragraph under No. 82.

The beginnings of an Imperial postal department for Italy date from Nerva or Trajan, but it was not till the time of Hadrian that it was properly organized under a *praefectus vehiculorum* (Hirschfeld, *Verwaltungsbcamten*, p. 193). The earliest evidence probably is *C. I. L.* x. 6976 = *D.* 1434.

p. 108. No. 84, l. 7. *Beneficiarius consularis.* The title of *consularis* was older than the second century, and was used in ordinary language of governors who had been consuls (e. g. Tac. *Agr.* 14), their *beneficiarii* being usually described as *beneficiarii consularis.*

p. 109. No. 85, which is now *C. I. L.* xiii. 8830. *Roman Occupation of Frisia.*

Another memorial of the presence of Rome in Frisia was found in 1917 in the same district in the form of a wood tablet inscribed with a contract for the sale of an ox by a Frisian to a Roman, Gargilius Secundus, which begins: 'Gargilius Secundus n(ummis) cxv a S[t]el[o] Riiperii Beeoso vil(l)a Lopetei rite uti l(icet) bovem emi'. Then follow the names of two centurions as witnesses, and a date by consuls (*suffecti*), C. Fufius (?) and Cn. Minicius. Cn. Minicius Faustinus was *cos. suff.* in 116.

P. F. Girard, *Textes de Droit Romain* (5th ed., Paris, 1923), p. 848, who dates it before A. D. 61.

Mnemosyne, N. S. xlv. (1917), 341; xlvi (1918), 201; *Jahreshefte des Oest. Arch. Inst.* xxiii (1926), 331.

p. 113. *Dalmatia.*

According to Ritterling (*Legio*, 1619) the reduction of the garrison to one legion dates from A. D. 57, when the VII Claudia was sent to Moesia to replace the IV Scythica, which had gone to Syria; but Filow (*Klio*, Beiheft vi. 21 f.) thinks that the seventh was transferred in A. D. 62.

p. 114. No. 90. Introductory note.

Mommsen's theory of the 'iteration of the primipilate' has now been replaced by the account of Von Domaszewski (*Rangordnung*, 113–115) showing that it was the highest rank of the *militia equestris*, usually coming after tribunates in the garrison of Rome (e. g. *D.* 2726: *T. Pontius Sabinus trib. coh. III vig., coh. XIIII urb., coh. II praet., p(rimus) p(ilus) II, proc. provinc. Narbonens.*, where other instances are cited). In the case of Atticus, tribune only of a praetorian cohort, the two special *praefecturae* which he held were probably regarded as equivalents of the two other tribunates. He was then qualified for the equestrian administrative posts. See also A. Stein, *Der römische Ritterstand* (Munich, 1927), 148 ff.; H. M. D. Parker, *The Roman Legions*, 204.

p. 115. *Moesia and the Lower Danube Provinces.*

The legatus of A. D. 6, described in Dio Cass. lv. 29. 3, as (Aulus) Καικίνας Σεουῆρος ὁ τῆς πλησιοχώρου Μυσίας ἄρχων, may have held only a special military command analogous to that of the two Germanies (see

p. 108 and cf. Von Premerstein, *Oest. Jahresheft* i, Beiblatt, 161 ff.; Ritterling, *Legio*, 1218-19, 1234). But by A. D. 9 the province will have been formed, though its organization may have taken some time to complete.

The *praefecturae* mentioned in No. 90 as held by Atticus do not necessarily imply that the organization was still in a rudimentary stage, for such continued to exist in long-established provinces where there remained *enclaves* of less civilized tribes, which had not reached the stage of city life, and were governed by military officers promoted to equestrian rank. For Dalmatia under Nero this is illustrated by *C. I. L.* ix. 2564, partly cited on p. 115 ; a dedication in A.D. 75 to Vespasian *ex testam[ento . . .] Marcelli centurionis leg. XI Cl[aud(iae), pr]aef(ecti) civitatis Maeze[iorum? et civit(atis) Daesit]iatium.*

p. 116. *Province of Thrace.*

Under Tiberius Thrace remained a client state, though a Roman 'Political Resident' acted as *tutor.* Tac. *Ann.* ii. 67. The annexation was definitely made by Claudius in A. D. 46, probably on the death of Rhoemetalces without heirs (Eusebius, *Chron.* 2062 = A. D. 46 : Θράκη ἀπὸ τοῦδε τοῦ χρόνου ἐπαρχία ἐχρημάτισε βασιλεύουσα πρίν).

pp. 117-120. No. 93.

The general result of recent discussion as to the meaning and date of the reduction of the forces under Plautius Aelianus, mentioned in No. 93, ll. 14, 15, has been to confirm the view adopted in the text (p. 119) that it refers to the transfer of the Fifth Legion to the East in A.D. 62 for Corbulo's Armenian campaign (p. 126). It is true that the Fourth Legion (which with the Fifth formed the original army of Moesia; see No. 91, p. 115) was also sent to the East in A.D. 57; but, though ultimately employed in the Armenian campaign, it went in the first instance to Syria, not to Armenia (cf. Tac. *Ann.* xv. 6. 5 of A.D. 62). Either then, or on the transfer of the Fifth Legion in A.D. 62, the Seventh Legion was moved to Moesia (see p. 113).

The succession of the governors of Moesia which can be inferred from the documents quoted in a Greek inscription from Histrus or Istrus in the Dobrudja (*Supplementum Epigraphicum Graecum*, i (Leyden, 1923), No. 329), as emended by Dessau (reading Αἰλιανῷ for Αἰμιλιανῷ), makes it probable that Fl. Sabinus was legatus A.D. 53-60, and that he was immediately succeeded by Plautius. In favour of this is the fact that Plautius, who was proconsul of Asia under Nero, probably in 55-6, was not likely to be appointed to Moesia immediately.

Dessau, *Oest. Jahreshefte*, xxiii (1926), Beiblatt, 346-358. Cf. his *Gesch. d. röm. Kais.* ii, pt. 1. 211, n. 6. Ritterling, *Legio*, 1559, 1574, 1619. Filow, Die Legionen der Provinz Moesia, *Klio*, Beiheft vi.

pp. 117-120. No. 93. *Roman policy in the Euxine lands under Nero.*

' The expedition of Plautius to the Crimea led to a temporary limitation of the semi-independence of the Bosporan kingdom, as may be legitimately inferred from the coin of A. D. 62-3 (p. 119) with the heads of

divus Claudius and Nero, accompanied by the monogram Νέρ(ων) Κ(αῖσαρ) ;
but it is likely that the king was reduced to the position of a Roman
procurator rather than deposed. Cotys himself, indeed, may have been
dead. A coin of A.D. 68–9, said to bear his monogram (*Zeitschr. f. Num.*,
iv (1877), 305), has been quoted to show that he was back in his old
position by that year; but there is little doubt that it has been incorrectly
described, and really belongs to his successor Rhescuporis. Nero's action
in the North must be correlated with his almost simultaneous annexation
of the Pontic regions in the South, and also with his projected campaign
against the Sarmatian Alani (not Albani), on the north of the Caucasus,
for which preparations were on foot in A.D. 66. The campaigns of Plautius
and Corbulo's reports from Armenia (cf. Plin. *H. N.* vi. 30 and 40) had,
no doubt, awakened the Roman government to a sense of the Sarmatian
peril, and Nero's intention seems to have been to secure control of the
Black Sea coastlands. On Nero's policy see E. Täubler, " Zur Geschichte
der Alanen" in *Klio* ix (1909), 14 ff.; Rostovtzeff, "Pontus, Bithynia
and the Bosporus " in *Annual Br. Sch. Athens*, xxii (1916–18), 1–22, and
his *Iranians and Greeks in S. Russia* (Oxford, 1922), 117 ff., 152 f.
W. Schur's elaborate discussion of Nero's Eastern policy in *Klio*, Beiheft
xv (1923), contains views which seem to me fanciful.' [J. G. C. A.]

p. 128. No. 98. *Camp of the Third Legion in Africa.*

Newly discovered milestones on the road made by Asprenas in A.D. 14
show that Theveste is too far south to have been the starting-point, and
it is practically certain that the head-quarters of the Third Legion under
the Early Empire were at Ammaedara (Haïdra), about twenty-five miles
to the north-east, where epitaphs of soldiers have been found of an earlier
date than those from Theveste. See De Pachtère in *Comptes Rendus de
l'Acad. des Inscr. &c.*, 1916, 273 ff.; Gsell, *Inscriptions Latines de
l'Algérie* (Paris, 1922), 286.

p. 130, 2nd par. Though the province was not divided, the Imperial
legatus exercised the civil power in and around the districts where troops
were quartered. Mommsen, *Gesammelte Schriften*, viii. 134 ; Gsell,
op. cit., p. ix.

p. 132. *The Roman Army in Egypt.*

The fact that P. Anicius Maximus had held the primipilate only once
shows that he cannot have been more than the *praefectus castrorum* of
the Egyptian army, not its commander. Under the Early Empire each
legion in Egypt had its *praefectus* who had been *primipilus iterum*
(*D.* 2687), the camp prefect being a simple *primipilus*. After the two
legions were quartered together they had in peace-time a single *praefectus
castrorum*, who in the second half of the first century was taken from the
primipili iterum and replaced the prefects of the legions, ranking
immediately after the Prefect of Egypt.

Von Domaszewski, *Rangordnung*, 120 f. J. Lesquier, ' L'armée romaine
d'Égypte' in *Mém. Inst. Fr. d'Arch. Orient. du Caire*, 1918, 119–132.
Parker, *Legions*, 204.

BIBLIOGRAPHY AND ABBREVIATIONS

B. M. C. Emp. i = *Coins of the Roman Empire in the British Museum.* Vol. i, Augustus to Vitellius. By H. Mattingly (London, For the Trustees, 1923).

B. M. C. Rep. = *Coins of the Roman Republic in the British Museum.* By H. A. Grueber (3 vols., London, 1910).

Bruns, *Fontes.* C. G. Bruns, *Fontes Iuris Romani Antiqui*, 7th ed. by O. Gradenwitz (Tübingen, 1909–12).

C. I. L. = *Corpus Inscriptionum Latinarum*, &c. (Berlin, from 1863 onwards). For contents see the treatises of Cagnat, Sandys, &c., and especially L. Perret, *Les Inscriptions romaines, Bibliographie pratique* (Paris, 1924).

Cohen = H. Cohen, *Description historique des monnaies frappées sous l'Empire romain communément appelées Médailles Impériales*, 2nd. ed. Paris and London, vol. i, 1880, vol. ii, 1882.

D. = H. Dessau, *Inscriptiones Latinae Selectae*, 3 vols. (Berlin, 1892–1916).

A. Von Domaszewski. *Die Rangordnung des römischen Heeres.* Bonner Jahrbücher, Heft 117, 1908.

Eckhel. Jos. Eckhel, *Doctrina numorum veterum*, vol. vi, 2nd ed., Vienna, 1828.

O. Hirschfeld. *Die kaiserlichen Verwaltungsbeamten bis auf Diocletian*, 2nd ed., Berlin, 1905.

J. R. S. = *Journal of Roman Studies* (Society for the Promotion of Roman Studies, London, from 1911).

Th. Mommsen. *Römisches Staatsrecht*, vols. ii and iii (Leipzig, 3rd edition, 1887, 1888). (*St. R.*).

—— *Res Gestae divi Augusti ex monumentis Ancyrano et Apolloniensi*, 2nd edition, Berlin, 1883.

—— *The Provinces of the Roman Empire from Caesar to Diocletian*, London, 1909.

Ritterling, *Legio.* Article by E. Ritterling on the Roman Legions from Augustus to Diocletian in vol. xii (1925) of Pauly-Wissowa, *Realencyclopädie der classischen Altertumswissenschaft* (Stuttgart, 1894 and onwards), cols. 1211–1829.

W. = *Exempla Inscriptionum Latinarum*, by G. Wilmanns (Berlin, 1873).

ABBREVIATIONS

[not explained in the text]

AVG	Augustus.
C	Gaius.
CN	Gnaeus.
COS	Consul.
D	Decimus.
D	Dedit.
D · M	Dis Manibus.
F	Filius, filia.
IMP	Imperator.
L	Libertus.
L	Lucius.
LEG	Legatus.
LEG	Legio.
M	Marcus.
M · P	Millia passuum.
N	Nepos.
N	Numerius.
P	Publius.
P · M	Pontifex Maximus.
P · P	Pater Patriae.
P · R	Populus Romanus.
PR	Praetor.
Q	Quaestor.
Q	Quintus.
S · C	Senatus consulto.
SEX	Sextus.
S · F	Sacris faciundis.
S · P · Q · R	Senatus Populusque Romanus.
T	Titus.
TI, TIB	Tiberius.

PART I.

AUGUSTUS.

B.C. 31–A.D. 14.

I. THE VICTORY OF OCTAVIANUS, AND THE FOUNDATION OF THE PRINCIPATE.

The Triumph in B.C. 29.

I.

C. I. L. vi. 873. Found in the Forum at Rome, near the Temple of Castor. The date is B.C. 29.

SENATVS · POPVLVSQVE · ROMANVS
IMP · CAESARI · DIVI · IVLI · F · COS · QVINCT
COS · DESIGN · SEXT · IMP · SEPT
REPVBLICA · CONSERVATA

2.

B. M. C. Emp. i, Aug. 656. Eckhel, vi. 88. Aureus of B.C. 27. The representations are explained by *Mon. Anc.* 6. 16, quoted on p. 4, and cf. Babelon, *Monnaies de la République*, p. 311, No. 1; Cohen, i. p. 116, No. 385. Several coins of Augustus with *ob cives servatos* refer to the same occasion.

Obverse. CAESAR COS. VII. CIVIBVS SERVATEIS. Head of Augustus.

Reverse. AVGVSTVS S. C. Eagle holding a wreath, between two boughs of laurel.

Whatever may have been the form of the monument with

B

which No. 1 was orig⁻…ally connected, there can be little
doubt that it was intended to be a record of the great event
of B.C. 29—the triple Triumph of Octavianus.   The view
here presented of Octavianus as the saviour of the Roman
Commonwealth is explained by the fear, prevalent before
the battle of Actium, that Antonius would transfer the
centre of power from Rome to Alexandria, as part of his
scheme for a restored Hellenistic Monarchy (cf. p. 21).
Dio Cass. 50. 4 : ἐπίστευσαν ... ὅτι, ἂν κρατήσῃ, τήν τε πόλιν
σφῶν τῇ Κλεοπάτρᾳ χαριεῖται καὶ τὸ κράτος ἐς τὴν Αἴγυπτον
μεταθήσει.   Cf. 49. 40. 3, 50. 3. 5, for other allusions to
Alexandria.   Among contemporary references cf. Hor. 1 *C.*
37. 6 : *Capitolio regina dementes ruinas, funus et imperio
parabat.*   Cf. 3. 3. 20, 57 sqq.

The *corona civica* (No. 2) conferred on Augustus in B.C. 27
(cf. No. 4 on which Mommsen remarks 'qui scripsit fastos
Praenestinos ... minus proprie rem explicavit' *Res Gest.
D. Aug.* 151) is explained by his own words (*Mon. Anc.*
1. 14): *victorque omnibus* [? *superstiti*]*bus civibus peperci.*   Cf.
Dio Cass. 53. 16. 4 : τό τε τὰς δάφνας πρὸ τῶν βασιλείων αὐτοῦ
προτίθεσθαι, καὶ τὸ τὸν στέφανον τὸν δρύινον ὑπὲρ αὐτῶν ἀρτᾶσθαι,
τότε οἱ ὡς καὶ ἀεὶ τούς τε πολεμίους νικῶντι καὶ τοὺς πολίτας
σώζοντι ἐψηφίσθη.   Pliny, *H. N.* 16. 8 : (*Augustus coronam*)
civicam a genere humano accepit, is thinking rather of Actium
as the end of the civil wars.

Mommsen, *Res Gestae D. Augusti,* 149-151.   *Sitzungsberichte der k. preuss.
Akademie der Wissenschaften zu Berlin,* 1889 (*Festrede*), 27-29.

Annexation of Egypt: B.C. 30.

3.

C. I. L. vi. 701.   On the obelisk of the Piazza del Popolo, Rome.   The inscription is repeated on both the north and south faces of the pedestal.   The obelisk
was erected by Augustus on the *spina* of the Circus Maximus, where it was
unearthed in 1587 by Sixtus V, who had it moved to its present position.   Its
fellow, with a similar inscription (*C. I. L.* vi. 702), stands on Monte Citorio

near its original site in the Campus Martius. Both are described by Pliny, *H. N.* 36. 71.

*i*MP · CAESAR · DĪVĪ · F

AVGVSTVS

PONTIFEX · MAXIMVS

*i*MP · X̄II · COS · X̄I · TRIB · POT · X̄IV

5   AEGVPTO · IN · POTESTÁTEM

POPVLĪ · ROMÁNĪ · REDÁCTÁ

*s*OLĪ · DÓNUM · DEDIT

Mon. Anc. 5. 24 : Aegyptum imperio populi [Ro]mani adieci.

This monument was erected in B.C. 10, twenty years after the annexation of Egypt; but for purposes of historical illustration it may be taken as a contemporary record of an event which, as Mommsen says (*Provinces*, ii. 233), was coincident both in point of time and of organic connection with the organisation of the Principate. It will be noticed that the annexation of Egypt is spoken of here (ll. 5, 6) in precisely the same way as in the Ancyran Monument (cf. *Mon. Anc.* 5. 9 : *omnium prov*[*inciarum populi Romani*] *quibus finitimae fuerunt gentes quae n*[*on parerent imperio nos*]*tro fines auxi* where the special reference is to the *provinciae Caesaris*). The reasons which caused Egypt to be administered on a different system from that of the ordinary provinces, are described by Tacitus, *Ann.* 2. 59. 4 : *Augustus . . . seposuit Aegyptum ne fame urgeret Italiam quisquis eam provinciam claustraque terrae ac maris quamvis levi praesidio adversum ingentes exercitus insedisset. Hist.* 1. 11 : *Aegyptum copiasque quibus coerceretur iam inde a divo Augusto equites Romani obtinent loco regum: ita visum expedire provinciam aditu difficilem, annonae fecundam, superstitione ac lascivia discordem et mobilem, insciam legum, ignaram magistratuum, domi retinere.*

The Foundation of the Principate, B.C. 27.

4.

C. I. L. i. p. 312. Entry for Jan. 13 in the *Fasti Praenestini.* For the arrangement of the Calendars see Introduction, p. xvii. The first notice is too fragmentary to be restored. The restoration of the second is made possible by the passage from the Ancyran Monument quoted below.

E EID N̄͡P

PVTA
ID · ES
NON
AL

CORONA · QVERN*a uti super ianuam domus. imp. caesaris*
AVGVSTI · PONER*etur senatus decrevit quod rem publicam*
P · R · REST*i*TVI*t*

Mon. Anc. 6. 13 : in consulatu sexto et septimo, b[ella ubi civil]ia exstinxeram per consensum universorum [potitus rerum omn]ium, rem publicam ex mea potestate in senat[us populique Romani a]rbitrium transtuli. Quo pro merito meo Senatu[s consulto Aug(ustus) appe]llatus sum et laureis postes aedium mearum v[estiti publice coronaq]ue civica super ianuam meam fixa est.

The catch-word *restituta respublica* is often repeated in some form or other by the contemporaries of Augustus. Cf. Ovid, *Fast.* 1. 589: *redditaque est omnis populo provincia nostro.* Velleius, 2. 89. 3 : (after Actium) *restituta vis legibus, iudiciis auctoritas, senatui maiestas, imperium magistratuum ad pristinum redactum modum . . . prisca illa et antiqua rei publicae forma revocata. C. I. L.* vi. 1527 (*Elogium Turiae*) d. 25: *pacato orbe terrarum res*[*titut*]*a republica.* By the side of these passages and of the words of Augustus in the Ancyran Monument, may be placed the legend on a cistophorus of B.C. 28 (Eckhel, vi. 83): *imp. Caesar divi f. cos. VI, libertatis p. R. vindex,* with *Pax* on the reverse. The reference in every case is to the surrender by Octavianus in B.C. 27 of the constituent power conferred on him and

his colleagues in the Triumvirate in B.C. 43. On the resignation of the sole surviving mandatory of that power,
the Government of the State once more constitutionally
belonged to the Senatus Populusque Romanus, and this
implied the restoration of (1) the regular organs of the
Constitution—the Comitia and Judicia, and (2) the government of the Senate and People in the provinces, including
the command of the armies of the State. But while the
Roman Commonwealth was restored, the position of Octavianus himself was now constitutionally defined, and hence
later writers insist, in connection with the events of B.C. 28–27,
not on the *restitutio rei publicae* but on the foundation of the
Principate. Dio Cass. 52. 1: ἐκ δὲ τούτου μοναρχεῖσθαι αὖθις
ἀκριβῶς ἤρξαντο. Tacitus, *Ann.* 3. 28. 3: *sexto demum consulatu Caesar Augustus, potentiae securus, quae triumviratu
iusserat abolevit deditque iura quis pace et principe uteremur.*
Eutropius, 7. 8 : *ex eo rempublicam per quadraginta et quattuor
annos solus obtinuit.* So Strabo, though a contemporary of
Augustus, writing (not after A.D. 23) for the Greek half of
the Empire says (17. 3. 25, p. 840): ἡ πατρὶς ἐπέτρεψεν αὐτῷ τὴν
προστασίαν τῆς ἡγεμονίας.

The essential feature of the position created for Octavianus
in B.C. 27 was the tenure of the Consulship with extended
powers. While the custom of the later Republic restricted
the acting Consul to Rome and Italy, that restriction was
now, in his case, abolished, and moreover for the next ten
years his Consulships were to be continuous. With this
position the following powers were combined. (1) The government of those provinces (except Africa) in which an army was
required (Dio Cass. 53. 12, 13. Suet. *Aug.* 47). (2) The sole
command of the army (Dio Cass. 53. 12. 3: αὐτὸς δὲ δὴ μόνος
καὶ ὅπλα ἔχῃ καὶ στρατιώτας τρέφῃ). (3) The right of declaring
war and making peace, i.e. the control of the foreign policy
of the State (Strabo, 17. 3. 25, p. 840: πολέμου καὶ εἰρήνης
κατέστη κύριος διὰ βίου. Cf. No. 70. Dio Cass. 53. 17. 5). All

these powers were extensions of his position as acting Consul, and his *imperium* would be constitutionally described as *consulare* (cf. Tac. *Ann.* 1. '2: *consulem se ferens*). Such a combination of powers did not differ in principle from arrangements previously made under the Republic, and Augustus was able to say with truth (*Mon. Anc. Gr.* 3. 17): ἀρχὴν οὐδεμ[ία]ν πα[ρὰ τὰ πά]τρ[ια] ἔ[θ]η διδομένην ἀνεδεξάμην.

> Mommsen, *Res Gestae Divi Aug.* 145-149. *Staatsrecht*, ii. 745, 870.
> Prof. Pelham, *Journal of Philology*, xvii. (1888), 32-36.

The Revised Constitution of B.C. 23.

5.

> *C. I. L.* i. p. 472, vi. 2014. 14-17. xiv. 2240. Fragment of the *Fasti Feriarum Latinarum* for B. C. 23, found in the ruins of the Temple of Jupiter Latiaris on the summit of the Mons Albanus, where the annual celebration took place. Now in the Museum at Naples. The form of the restoration is based on the more perfect fragments. The day of the month in l. 2 is illegible. The date of the abdication is suggested by the regular time for a change of Consuls at the beginning of the second half of the year. Cf. *Fasti Cons. C. I. L.* i. p. 442. *St. R.* ii. 83, 84.

imp. caesare xi	*c*N · PISONE · COS
l(atinae) (feriae) f(uerunt)	· IVL
imp.	*caes*AR · IN MONTE FVIT
*k(alendis) iul(iis)(?) imp. ca*ESAR	· COS ABDICAVIT

6.

> *B. M. C. Emp.* i. 235. Cf. Eckhel, vi. 91, 92. As of B.C. 6.

Obverse. CAESAR AVGVST. PONT. MAX. TRIBVNIC. POT. Head of Augustus.

Reverse. A. LICIN. NERVA SILIAN(*us*) III VIR A(*uro*) A(*rgento*) A(*ere*) F(*lando*) F(*eriundo*) round S. C.

The resignation of the Consulship by Augustus in B.C. 23 (with No. 5, cf. Dio Cass. 53. 32. 3: ἀπεῖπε τὴν ὑπατείαν ἐς Ἀλβανὸν ἐλθών) was a turning-point in the history of the Principate, for it was thereby severed from any essential

connection with the Republican magistracies. The reason
for the step must have been the desire to put the Constitution of the Principate on a consistent and permanent basis
(cf. Suet. *Aug.* 28: *ita mihi salvam ac sospitem rem publicam
sistere in sua sede liceat* ... *ut optimi status auctor dicar, et
moriens ut feram mecum spem mansura in vestigio suo funda-
menta rei publicae quae iecero*), for though there were practical
inconveniences connected with the Emperor's tenure of the
Consulship, such as the presence of a colleague, annual
election, the danger of rousing the hostility of the Senatorial
order by appropriating one of the two highest prizes of the
official career, yet they were hardly felt at the time. How
little e.g. the Senatorial grievance suggested above was
appreciated, may be seen from the fact that more than once
in the years immediately following B.C. 23, only one Consul
was elected and the other place left vacant in the hope of
inducing Augustus to take it (Dio Cass. 54. 6. 2, 10).

By resigning the Consulship Augustus did not lose his
command of the army and of his own provinces (his *imperium* being now described as *proconsulare*), except that
(1) instead of having as Consul an *imperium maius* over Pro-
consuls in the Senatorial provinces, he now, as one Proconsul among many, had only an *imperium aequum*, and
(2) this was no longer valid in Rome. In regard to both
points his old position was at once restored to him by the
Senate. Dio Cass. 53. 32. 5: τήν τε ἀρχὴν τὴν ἀνθύπατον ἐσαεὶ
καθάπαξ ἔχειν ὥστε μήτε ἐν τῇ ἐσόδῳ τῇ εἴσω τοῦ πωμηρίου κατα-
τίθεσθαι αὐτὴν μήτ' αὖθις ἀνανεοῦσθαι, καὶ ἐν τῷ ὑπηκόῳ τὸ πλεῖον
τῶν ἑκασταχόθι ἀρχόντων ἰσχύειν ἐπέτρεψεν. But though Augustus did not shrink from exhibiting in Rome the outward
sign of his *proconsulare imperium*—the Praetorian Guard, it
was nevertheless desirable that he should appear there as
the holder of a constitutional position as nearly as possible
equivalent to the Consulship. The only institution which
offered such a position was the Tribunate of the Plebs, in its

origin a kind of counter-Consulship, in power the rival, and in some ways the superior of the older magistracy. Augustus could not become a *tribunus plebis* for he was a Patrician and it was part of his system to remain one, and moreover he would have been subjected to the restrictions of colleagues and annual election. But the powers and privileges of the Tribunate had been already given to him for life in B.C. 36 under the title of *tribunicia potestas*, and this power, hitherto used by him only *ad tuendam plebem* (Tac. *Ann.* 1. 2), was now brought into prominence, and the intention of making it equivalent to the resigned Consulship shown by an annual character being given to it (i.e. its years are numbered beginning with B.C. 23. No. 6).

Augustus would still have lost some of the prestige and of the privileges attached to the Consulship, if these had not been made up to him in other ways. By his *tribunicia potestas* he could convene the Senate and bring business before it, but only after Consuls and Praetors. He was now given precedence over every one in this respect (Dio Cass. 53. 32. 5, 54. 3. 3), and he was moreover reinstated in all the external privileges of his old position. (Dio Cass. 54. 10. 5: ταῖς δώδεκα ῥάβδοις ἀεὶ καὶ πανταχοῦ χρῆσθαι, καὶ ἐν μέσῳ τῶν ἀεὶ ὑπατευόντων ἐπὶ τοῦ ἀρχικοῦ δίφρου καθίζεσθαι.)

The essential merit of the *tribunicia potestas* was that it gave the Emperor an exceptional position (Tac. *Ann.* 3. 56. 2: *summi fastigii vocabulum Augustus repperit, ne regis aut dictatoris nomen adsumeret ac tamen appellatione aliqua cetera imperia praemineret*). The settlement of B.C. 23 was final, and the power of every Roman Emperor was cast in this mould until the development of pure Monarchy in the fourth century. For the single act by which this and the other powers were conferred on the successors of Augustus see No. 70.

Mommsen, *Staatsrecht*, ii. 871, 896.
Prof. Pelham, *Journal of Philology*, xvii. (1888), 36.

II. THE ORGANISATION OF THE PROVINCES.

Spain.

7.

C. I. L. vi. 31267. *D.* 103. Marble base. Apparently connected with some object of gold which stood in the Forum of Augustus, on the site of which the inscription was found. Cf. Vell. 2. 39. 2: *divus Augustus praeter Hispanias aliasque gentis, quarum titulis forum eius praenitet.* The formula at the end is: *auri p(ondo) c(entum).*

```
        IMP   ·   CAESARI
           AVGVSTO P P
        HISPANIA · VLTERIOR
          BAETICA · QVOD
  5    BENEFICIO  EIVS  ET
        PERPETVA CVRA
      PROVINCIA    PACATA
          EST  ·  AVRI
             P · C
```

8.

C. I. L. ii. 4868. The fourth milestone from Bracara on the road to Asturica. The date is A. D. 11-12.

```
  IMP · CAESAR · DIVI · F · AVG
 PONT · MAXIMVS · IMP · XV · CONSVL
   XIII · TRIB · POTEST · XXXIV · PA
     TER · PATRIAE · BRAC
          I · I · I · I
```

9.

C. I. L. ii. 4701. One of a number of milestones from the Via Augusta, now at Cordova. Ianus Augustus is explained by *C. I. L.* ii. 4721: *ab arcu unde incipit Baetica viam Aug(ustam) [restituit]*, on a milestone of Domitian from the same road.   Augustus was Cos. xiii in B.C. 2.   Ɫ is an older form of L from the Chalcidian ψ(χ).

IMP · CAESAR · DIVĪ · F
AVGVSTVS · COS · X̄III · TRIB
POTEST · X̄XI · PONTIF · MAX
Á · BAETE · ET · IANO · AVGVST
5   AD · OCEANVM
ɫXIIII

The pacification of Spain referred to in No. 7 was the result of the long struggle with the tribes in the North-West (Cantabri and Astures. B.C. 26–19). That struggle left permanent traces on the arrangements of the whole country, but more particularly in the northern province which the Emperor retained in his own hands, and where it was thought necessary to maintain a force of three legions (originally IV Macedonica, VI Victrix, X Gemina) down to the time of Claudius. The only evidence however of a rising after Augustus is the inscription, dated A.D. 66, of M. Vettius Valens, who among other distinctions was *donis donato ob res prosper(e) gest(as) contra Astures.   C. I. L.* xi. 395 = *D. 2648.* As the valley of the Ebro formed the regular approach to the districts of the North-West, it was natural that the centre of power should be transferred from Carthago Nova to Tarraco which had been the basis of operations during the war (Dio Cass. 53. 25. 7), and which now became, first the northern, and finally the only capital of the province (its position is indicated by the fact that it was the meeting place of the *concilium provinciae,* Tac. *Ann.* 1. 78. *C. I. L.* ii. p. 540; and cf. Strabo, 3. 4. 7, p. 159 : Ταρράκων . . . οὐχ ἧττον εὐανδροῦσα νυνὶ τῆς Καρχηδόνος. πρὸς γὰρ τὰς τῶν ἡγεμόνων ἐπιδημίας εὐφυῶς ἔχει καὶ ἔστιν ὥσπερ μητρόπολις οὐ τῆς ἐντὸς Ἰβηρος μόνον ἀλλὰ καὶ τῆς ἐκτὸς τῆς πολλῆς).   No. 8 belongs to one of the roads made by Augustus to connect the Roman centres in the dangerous north-western districts (Asturica Augusta, Bracarà Augusta, Lucus Augusti) with one another.

The most important road in the south of Spain was the Via Augusta which followed the valley of the Baetis (No. 9), and ultimately joined the coast road to Italy. Originally it passed through Carthago Nova, and as late as B.C. 7 Augustus was developing this route (*C. I. L.* ii. 4936–4938 milestones found between Carthago and Castulo); but after the shifting of the official centre of Hispania Citerior to Tarraco, the road on passing the frontier of Baetica took a direct line to the coast at Valentia leaving Carthago untouched. The old route through the latter city is indicated in Polybius, 3. 39. 6–8, the new and shorter one in Strabo, 3. 4. 9, p. 160.

Mommsen, *Provinces*, i. 66, 74.

Gallia Narbonensis.

10.

C. I. L. xii. 1371. Sepulchral inscription built into the doorway of a Church at Entrechaux near Vaison (Vasio). The pagus of which Q. Pompeius was *praefectus* ,l. 4) seems to have been called by the name of its inhabitants. No perfect instance of *praetor Vasiensium Vocontiorum* has been preserved, but the form is confirmed by the many cases in which Vasienses Vocontii is used as the full name of the civitas. Cf. No. 60 and *C. I. L.* xii. p. 161.

Q POM*peio* . . *f.*
  VOLT . . . . .
AEDILI   *vocont.* ?
PRAEF · BO . . . . .
5   TIOR · $\overline{\text{PR}}$ · V*as. voc.* ?
FLAMINI · D*ivi aug.*
PONTIF · DEA*e aug.* ?
POMPEIA · *Secunda* ?
  FILIA
10   PATRI ·* OPT*imo*
   EX *m*ODIC*itate sua*

Q. Pom[*peio* . . . . *f*(*ilio*)] *Volt*(*inia*) (*tribu*) . . . ., *acdili* [*Vocont*(*iorum*)], *praef*(*ecto*) *Bo* . . . . *tior*(*um*), *pr*(*actori*)

V[*as*(*iensium*) *Voc*(*ontiorum*)], *flamini d*[*ivi Aug*(*usti*)], *pontif*(*ici*) *dea*[*e Aug*(*ustae*)], *Pompeia S*[*ecunda*] *filia patri
opt*[*imo*] *ex* [*m*]*odic*[*itate sua*].

II.

C. I. L. xii. 1376.   Found at a village near Vaison.   Now in the Museum at St.
Germain.   In l. 4 the more intelligible reading XLII has been adopted instead
of XIII.

<pre>
          D   ·   M
        VALERI · MAXIMI
        FIL · DEFVNCT · ANN ·
                  XLII
  5   PRAEF · VIGINTIVI
        RORVM   ·   PAGI
              DEOBENSIS
        VALERIA · MATER · ET ·
        CASS · EROS · MARĪVS
 10   EIVS
</pre>

D(*is*) *M*(*anibus*) *Valeri Maximi fil*(*i*) *defunct*(*i*) *ann*(*orum*)
XLII, praef(*ecti*) *vigintivirorum pagi Deobensis, Valeria
mater et Cass*(*ius*) *Eros maritus eius.*

12.

C. I. L. xii. 1028.   Votive inscription found at Avignon and now in the
Museum there. l. 2 : *pr*(*aetor*) *Volcar*(*um*).   Probably not much later than Caesar.

<pre>
    T ⊘ CARISIVS ⊘ T ⊘ F
    PR ⊘ VOLCAR ⊘ DAT
</pre>

13.

C. I. L. xii. 3215.   Found at Nîmes.

<pre>
    L · DOMITIO · L · F · VOL
    AXıOVNO · PR · IIĪI VIR · BIS
</pre>

L. Domitio L. f. Vol(*tinia*) (*tribu*) *Axiouno, pr*(*aetori*) *IIII
vir*(*o*) *bis.*

14.

C. I. L. xii. 3179. Found at Nîmes (Nemausus) and preserved there. Though the Sixteenth Legion, like the rest of the army of Upper Germany, did not join in the mutiny of A. D. 14 (Tac. *Ann.* 1. 31. 3) it received the same concessions as the legions of Lower Germany (Tac. *Ann.* 1. 37. 5: *pecunia et missio quamvis non flagitantibus oblata est*), and Festús may have been one of those who came under the regulation *missionem dari vicena stipendia meritis* (id. 36. 4). *Sui* in l. 7 is certain, and may be due to mere awkwardness of expression (*balneum gratuitum* occurs in *C. I. L.* xii. 594); but possibly, as suggested in the Corpus, it is a mistake of the stone-cutter's for *et balnei usum*. M̄ in l. 6 is for *modios*.

```
        TI · CAESARIS
        DIVI · AVG · F · AVGVSTI
       MĪLES · MISSICIVS · T · IVLIVS
       FÉSTVS · MILITÁVIT · ANNOS · XXV
5      IN · LEGIÓNE · X̄V̄I · DECRETO · DECVRION
       ACCEPIT · FRVMENTI · M̄ · L · BALNEVM ET
       SVI · GRATVITVM · IN · PERP · ET · AREAM · IN
       TER · DVÓS · TVRRÉS · PER · P · PVSONIVM · PERE
       GRINVM · ĪĪĪĪ · VIR · ET · X̄Ī · VIR · ADSIGNÁTAM
```

These inscriptions illustrate the different types of organisation which might exist within the same province, and more particularly, the different forms under which the process of Romanisation was carried on in the South of Gaul. The previously restricted province of Gallia Narbonensis was practically reconstituted by Caesar, who in B.C. 49 annexed the greater part of the territory of Massilia which included the trade routes to the coast of Gaul and the Rhone as high as Avennio, and laid the foundations of Roman organisation. The work was completed by Augustus in B.C. 27–15 (Dio Cass. 53. 22. 5, 54. 23. 7). For the relation between the province and the communities to which these inscriptions belong cf. Strabo, 4. 6. 4, p. 203 : Ἀλλόβριγες μὲν οὖν . . . ὑπὸ τοῖς στρατηγοῖς τάττονται τοῖς ἀφικνουμένοις εἰς τὴν Ναρβωνῖτιν, Οὐοκόντιοι δέ, καθάπερ τοὺς Οὐόλκας ἔφαμεν τοὺς περὶ Νέμαυσον, τάττονται καθ' αὑτούς.

The *civitas foederata* of the Vocontii (Plin. *H. N.* 3. 37) may be classed with the sixty-four *civitates* of the Tres Galliae (p. 17) as a case in which Rome did not impose her own institutions, but was content to leave the national constitution at work under Roman names and wait for a gradual process of assimilation. Here the tribal organisation was never replaced by the municipal. No preponderating town-centre was developed, and the canton was never absorbed in the territory of a great Roman or Latin city. Vasio was indeed the political capital (hence Vasienses Vocontii is used as a name for the whole *civitas*, v. sup.), but it had rivals in Lucus Augusti (Tac. *Hist.* 1. 66. 5. Cf. Pliny l. c.: *duo capita*), and Dea Augusta, the old religious centre of the canton, where, characteristically enough, the Celtic worship of Andarta maintained itself in a Roman dress (No. 10. 7). The case is to be contrasted with that of Nemausus, from the first the religious as well as the political centre of the canton of the Volcae, where besides favourable conditions developed great material prosperity. Moreover the constitution of the *civitas* retained many traces of the persistence of national organisation. There was indeed a Senate of the Roman municipal pattern, and the subordinate magistrates (*aediles* No. 10. 3) seem to belong to the same order of things ; but the chief magistracy was held by a single *praetor* (No. 10. 5), an arrangement which, differing essentially as it does from the Roman collegiate principle, may be a survival of the *vergobret* of pre-Roman times (Caes. *B. G.* 1. 16. 5: *Lisco qui summo magistratui praeerat quem vergobretum appellant Aedui qui creatur annuus et vitae necisque in suos habet potestatem*, cf. 7. 32. 3. Strabo, 4. 4. 3, p. 197). Further we learn from No. 11 that there was a body of *vigintiviri*, whether belonging to the *civitas* or the *pagus* is not clear, probably to the latter (*C. I. L.* xii. pp. 161,

162), but in any case no doubt a Celtic institution (cf. the *XI viri* at Nemausus, No. 14). For other Celtic survivals see Hirschfeld, *Gallische Studien*, 313–317, and *C. I. L.* xii. p. 162.

The cantons of the Allobroges and Volcae Arecomici on the other hand, starting with an organisation similar to that of the Vocontii, are replaced before long by the Latin colonies of Vienna and Nemausus. In the case of the former no traces of the transition have been preserved, but the earliest evidence of Latinisation among the Volcae (No. 12, 'Caesaris dictatoris aetate vix antiquiore,' *C. I. L.* xii. p. 381) still shows a *praetor Volcarum* like the *praetor Vocontiorum.* Here however Augustus founded at Nemausus, the old religious centre of the canton, a colony with Latin rights, governed by the regular college of four magistrates *IIII viri iure dicundo* or *ab aerario*, between whom and the *praetor Volcarum* the *praetores IIII viri* of No. 13 perhaps form a connecting link. The *XI viri* only known from No. 14 may be the survival of a pre-Roman institution. If so, there is a parallel to them in the *undecim primi* known in at least three protected native communities in Africa. In this new constitution of Nemausus the townships of the Volcae had no share, for they were treated as subject to the colony on the principle of 'attributio' explained on p. 38 (Plin. *H. N.* 3. 37: *oppida ignobilia XXIIII Nemausensibus adtributa*).

For the results of Romanisation in Gallia Narbonensis cf. Plinius, *H. N.* 3. 31: *agrorum cultu, virorum morumque dignatione, amplitudine opum, nulli provinciarum postferenda, breviterque Italia verius quam provincia.*

O. Hirschfeld, *Gallische Studien. Sitzungsberichte der k. Akad. der Wissen-schaften (Wien), Phil. Hist. Classe*, 1883. 271 and esp. 289 sqq. *Westdeutsche Zeitschrift*, viii. 119.

Mommsen, *Provinces*, i. 86 note.

The Three Gauls.

15.

Allmer, *Revue Épigraphique du Midi de la France*, ii. p. 456. (1889), No. 781. Desjardins, *Géographie de la Gaule Romaine*, i. p. 415, note 2. Fragment of a sepulchral inscription built into the wall of the Cathedral at Le Puy-en-Velay (Haute Loire), the ancient Anicium.

. . . . *conductor* (?)
FERRARIAR GVTVATER PRAEFECTVS COLON
QVI ANTE QVAM HIC QVIESCO LIBEROS MEOS
VTROSQ VIDI NONN FEROCEM FLAM · II̅ vIRVM^BIS

. . . .

16.

De Boissieu, *Inscriptions Antiques de Lyon*, p. 96. On two faces of the arch at Saintes, erected under Tiberius. For the *praefect fabrum* see p. 25. The last word is *d(edit)*. The Celtic name of the greatgrandfather is spelt *Epotsorovidus* on one face of the arch, and this may be correct.

C · IVLIVS · C · IVLI · OTVANEVNI · F · RVFVS · C · IVLI
· GEDEMONIS · NEPOS · EPOSTEROVIDI · PRON
SACERDOS · ROMAE · ET · AVGVSTI · AD · ARAM · QVAE
· EST · AD . CONFLVENTEM · PRAEFECTVS · FABRVM · D

17.

De Boissieu, *Inscriptions de Lyon*, p. 95. Found near Cahors (Cadurci) and now preserved there.

M · LVCTER*io*
LVCTERII · SEN*e*
CIANI · F · LEONI
OMNIBVS · HO
5 NORIBVS · IN · PA
TRIA · FVNCTO
SACERD · ARAE
AVG · INTER · CON
FLVENT · ARAR

10   ET · RHODANI
CIVITAS · CAD
OB · MERIT · EIVS
PVBL · POSVIT

*M. Lucter[io] Lucterii Sen[e]ciani f. Leoni, omnibus honori-
bus in patria functo, sacerd(oti) arae Aug(usti) inter confluent(es)
Arar(is) et Rhodani, civitas Cad(urcorum) ob merit(a) eius
publ(ice) posuit.*

The epigraphic evidence about the Three Gauls has not
yet been conveniently brought together, and therefore the
condition of the country cannot be illustrated with the ease
which is possible in the case of some parts of the Empire.
These inscriptions however illustrate two important facts in
the history of Roman Gaul.

(1) The organisation of the Three Gauls was based on the
recognition and regulation of the existing Gallic Communities (Tac. *Ann.* 3. 44: *quattuor et sexaginta Galliarum civitates*), an arrangement which left permanent traces in the
names of the town-centres which grew up in each *civitas.*
Here, therefore, in contrast to Gallia Narbonensis, no colonies
were founded by Augustus (notice the omission in *Mon. Anc.*
5. 35), and such as arose later were almost wholly in Germany. But by an exception which proves the rule, the
federal capital of the three provinces was a colony. It had
been founded in B.C. 43 by L. Munatius Plancus, but received a confirmation from Augustus with the title Augusta
(Colonia Copia Claudia Augusta, after Claudius). Accordingly it may have been at Lugudunum that the author of
No. 15 acted as *praefectus* in the absence or abeyance of the
regular magistrates (cf. No. 100), and that his son, Nonnius
Ferox, was *flamen Augustalis* (not to be confused with the
priesthood of the three provinces, Nos. 16 and 17, see p. 47),
and *duumvir* (all the offices are illustrated by another inscription, de Boissieu, p. 156 = *D.* 1441 = Allmer, *Lyon,* ii.

p. 117). The neighbourhood of the mines which he farmed
from the State no doubt explains the residence of the father
of Nonnius Ferox at Anicium. The mineral wealth of this
part of Gaul was sufficiently important to require, at least
in later times, the presence of a special office of the Fiscus
at Lugudunum, e.g. *C.I.L.* xiii. 1797 : *procurator ferrariarum,*
1808 = *D.* 1454 : *tabularius rationis ferrariarum.*

(2) The conjunction in No. 15 of a Roman magistracy
with a Celtic priesthood (*Gutuater* = the speaker, *vates,* according to D'Arbois de Jubainville : Desjardins, *Gaule,* ii. 721
note) illustrates the fact that by the side of the toleration
of national usages in Gaul a rapid process of Romanisation
went on. In No. 16 the transition can, as often, be followed
in the case of a single family. The oldest representative has a
purely Celtic name, and belongs at latest to the epoch of the
conquest. Apparently his son received Roman citizenship
from the conqueror, but in his case and in that of the next
generation a Latinised Celtic name is retained as cognomen.
Finally the Priest of the Three Gauls appears with a wholly
Roman name. No. 17 is an even more striking instance.
M. Lucterius Leo is evidently the descendant of that Lucterius who maintained at Uxellodunum one of the last
struggles for national independence in Gaul. Then as now,
the leaders of the Cadurci come from the same family ; but
while in the days of Caesar it heads the resistance to Rome,
under the Empire its traditional importance secures for its
representative the highest provincial dignity under the new
régime, the High-priesthood of the Three Gauls (cf. Hirtius,
B. G. 8. 32 : *in finibus consistunt Cadurcorum. Ibi cum
Lucterius apud suos cives . . . multum potuisset . . . magnam
apud barbaros auctoritatem haberet, oppidum Uxellodunum quod
in clientela fuerat eius . . . occupat).*

C. Jullian, Gallia, Paris, 1892.

Pannonia.

18.

C. I. L. iii. 4060.   Built into the church of a village near Pettau (Poetovio).
l. 2 : *Arn(ensi) (tribu)* ; l. 4 : *(centurio) leg(ionis)* &c.

```
        M · PETRONVS
        M · F · ARN · CLASSI
        CVS  ·  MARRVCNVS
        ᒣ LEG · VIII · AVG
   5    HIC · EST · CREMATVS
        OSSA · RELATA · DOMI
             ♂ ♀
        FRATER  ET  CONux
        . . . CA POSVerunt
```

This epitaph is one of the indications that under the early
Julian dynasty, the three legions (VIII Augusta, IX His-
pana, XV Apollinaris, Tac. *Ann.* 1. 23. 6) which then formed
the garrison of the frontier province of Pannonia or Illyricum
Inferius, were stationed not on the Danube but on the Drave.
Augustus indeed recognized the Danube as the political
boundary of the Empire (*Mon. Anc.* 5. 46 : *protulique fines
Illyrici ad r*[*ip*]*am fluminis Dan*[*u*]*i*), but there is a presump-
tion that a similar reason to that which kept the German
legions on the Rhine (viz. the need of a force to overawe
Gaul) would prevent the Pannonian legions from being moved
far from the scene of the national rising of A.D. 6–9.   Nothing
is known of the positions of the other two legions, but
No. 18 makes it highly probable that Poetovio was the
standing-camp of the Eighth before its departure for Moesia
under Nero (Tac. *Hist.* 1. 79. 8, 3. 10. *C. I. L.* iii. p. 482), and
this is confirmed by the fact that in A.D. 69 the Thirteenth
Legion, which took its place, was stationed there (Tac. *Hist.*
3. 1 : *Poetovionem in hiberna tertiae decimae legionis convene-
runt*).   It seems clear too from the orders given to the
governor of Pannonia in Tacitus, *Ann.* 12. 29. 2 : *legionem*

. . . *pro ripa componere*, that in A.D. 50 none of the legions
were stationed on the Danube. This does not exclude the
existence of military posts on the bank of the river (for
Carnuntum under Augustus see Velleius, 2. 109. 5) which was
also guarded by a flotilla (Tac. 12. 30. 3). See further
Mommsen, *Provinces*, i. 205 note, for possibility that the
Fifteenth Legion had been transferred to Carnuntum under
Claudius or Nero.

No. 18 has recently been confirmed by two more epitaphs from Pettau of
Italian soldiers (one a veteran) of the Eighth Legion. *Arch. Epigr. Mittheilungen
aus Oesterreich-Ungarn*, xv. (1892), 122.

The Eastern policy of Augustus.

19.

B. M. C. Emp. i, Aug. 647.   Eckhel, vi. 82.   Silver Quinarius of B. C. 29.

Obverse. CAESAR IMP. VII.   Head of Augustus.

Reverse. ASIA RECEPTA. Victory standing on the mystic *cista*,
holding a palm and crown.   A serpent on either side.

20.

B. M. C. Emp. i, Aug. 427.   Eckhel, vi. 101.   Aureus of Augustus.   On the
reverse a triumphal arch is represented upon which is Augustus in a quadriga
receiving the standards from two Parthians.   The date is B.C. 18–17.

Obv. S. P. Q. R. IMP. CAESARI AVG. COS. XI. TR.
POT. VI.   Head of Augustus.

Rev. CIVIB(*us*) ET SIGN(*is*) MILIT(*aribus*) A PART(*his*)
RECVP(*eratis*).

21.

B. M. C. Emp. i, Aug. 676.   Denarius of B. C. 19.   Cf. Mommsen, *Res Gestae*

Obverse. AVGVSTVS.   Head of Augustus.

Reverse. CAESAR DIV. F. ARMEN. CAPTA IMP. VIIII.   An
Armenian holding a spear and bow.

Mon. Anc. 5. 40: Parthos trium exercitum Roman[o]rum spolia et signa
re[ddere] mihi supplicesque amicitiam populi Romani petere coegi.

5. 24 : Armeniam maiorem interfecto rege eius Artaxe c[u]m possem facere

provinciam, malui maiorum nostrorum exemplo regn[u]m id Tigrani regis
Artavasdis filio, nepoti autem Tigranis regis, per T[i. Ne]ronem trad[er]e, qui
tum mihi priv[ig]nus erat. Et eandem gentem postea d[esc]iscentem et rebel-
lantem domit[a]m per Gaium filium meum regi Ario[barz]ani regis Medorum
Artaba[zi] filio regendam tradidi et post e[ius] mortem filio eius Artavasdi.
Quo [inte]rfecto [Tigra]ne[m], qui erat e regio genere Armeniorum oriundus
in id re[gnum] misi.

These coins mark two stages in the re-assertion by Augustus of the principle of Roman preponderance in Eastern
politics. Antonius had intended to re-assert it first by an
appeal to the sword, and ultimately perhaps by the conquest
of Parthia and the foundation of a Hellenistic Monarchy on
the model of that of the Seleucids (p. 2). Moreover he had,
in the same spirit, gone far towards bringing back in the
eastern provinces the state of things before the Roman conquest, by restoring the outlying territories of the Egyptian
Monarchy (esp. Palestine, Cyprus, Cyrene), and by creating
principalities for the children of Cleopatra, both at the
expense of Roman sovereignty in those parts (cf. Dio
Cass. 49. 32. 4, 41, and Mommsen, *Res Gest. D. Aug.* 118).
This policy was repudiated by Augustus. The great force
at his disposal after Actium was not used either to conquer
Parthia or even to extract from her a confession of inferi-
ority, but at the same time Roman supremacy west of the
Euphrates was completely restored (hence *Asia recepta* of
No. 19), and with the annexation of Egypt the last of the
great Hellenistic kingdoms disappeared.

Augustus however still had to settle the question of the restoration of Roman prestige, originally raised by the disaster
of Carrhae, and rendered more acute by the failure of Antonius in B.C. 36. Here, by making use of the difficulties
internal and external of Phraates, he achieved, at least temporarily, the same result that Caesar had intended to bring
about by force of arms. Perhaps it was the near prospect of
these difficulties which induced the Parthian king in B.C. 23
to come to terms with Augustus, and to promise to restore
the standards and captives (Dio Cass. 53. 33); certainly it

was their pressure which compelled him in B.C. 20 to carry out his part of the bargain, No. 20. One indication of the instability of the position of Phraates at this time is the break in his coinage beginning in the latter part of B.C. 23 and lasting for several years.

Augustus was not satisfied with a mere concession of the principle of Roman superiority on the part of Parthia, and at the same time that the standards were restored, Armenia, the land where the interests of Rome and Parthia came chiefly into collision, was brought back to the position of a Roman client-state to which it had been reduced by Pompeius in B.C. 66 (*Mon. Anc.* 5. 24), and No. 21 therefore speaks of it as included in the Empire (Mommsen, *Res Gestae*, 112). It was just here that the settlement of B.C. 20 failed, for the national party in Armenia found a natural rallying-point in Parthia, and in B.C. 1 Gaius Caesar had to be sent to the East to invest Ariobarzanes with the kingdom, just as Tiberius had invested Tigranes in B.C. 20; while to make the parallel complete, it was the internal troubles of Parthia which compelled Phraataces to accept the new arrangement (Dio Cass. 55. 10 a. 4), which was not more permanent than the former one. Before the death of Augustus, Armenia had once more gone over to the Parthian side. Cf. Tac. *Ann.* 2. 3. 2: (*Armenia*) *vacua tunc interque Parthorum et Romanas opes infida.* 2. 56.

Mommsen, *Res Gestae D. Augusti*, 109-118, 124-126. Section on Parthia by Prof. A. von Gutschmid in article *Persia, Encyclopaedia Britannica*, 9th ed. Prof. P. Gardner, *The Parthian Coinage*, p. 42 sqq.

Colonies of Augustus in Pisidia.

22.

C. I. L. iii. *Suppl.* 6974. Milestone from the site of Comama. The last word of l. 5 is very fragmentary. In the Corpus it is suggested that it may be *regalem.* The date is B. C. 6.

IMP CAESAR
DIVI *f.* AVGVS*tus pont*

MAXIM COS XI DeS

X̄I̅I̅ IMP XV TR *p*OT

5   XIIX VIAM . . . . .

CVRANTE · CORN

AQVILA LEG SVO

PRO PR FECIT

CXXII

This is the milestone from which Mommsen has inferred the date of the foundation of the Pisidian military colonies of Augustus. It being the policy of the Imperial Government to protect the existing (Hellenic) civilisation of the provinces of the East, without attempting to Latinise them, the Roman colonies there are, generally speaking, few and isolated (e. g. Berytus). But in the case of Pisidia there were special circumstances. The tribes which inhabited the mountain ranges between Lycia and Cilicia were practically untouched by Hellenism, and moreover they were a standing danger to peace. Here accordingly Augustus founded a series of colonies (*Mon. Anc. 5. 36*), the list of which has gradually been completed by the evidence of coins and inscriptions. Those known are, Antioch, Olbasa, Comama, Cremna, Parlais (probably at the south end of lake Caralitis), and Lystra. They formed a chain of garrisons which held the mountain tribes of Pisidia, Isauria, and Western Cilicia (the Homonadenses, Tac. *Ann.* 3. 48. 2) in check, and at the same time acted as civilising agencies. Antioch had a distinctively Latin character as is evidenced by the relatively large number of Latin inscriptions found there. Its connection with the other colonies as their centre is shown by No. 22, which, as Prof. Ramsay has pointed out, makes it probable that Antioch was the starting-point of the road (the number of miles exactly corresponds with that in the Tabula Peutingeriana between Antioch and Comama via Apollonia), and is further illustrated by the Greek inscription found near the site of Antioch (Sterrett, *Wolfe Expedition*, No. 352):

τὴν λαμπροτάτην Ἀντιοχέων Κολωνίαν ἡ λαμπροτάτη Λυστρέων
Κολωνία τὴν ἀδελφὴν τῷ τῆς Ὁμονοίας ἀγάλματι ἐτείμησεν.

Prof. Ramsay, *Geography of Asia Minor*, 46, 57, 390, 398. Mommsen.
Provinces, i. 334-337.

Syria under P. Sulpicius Quirinius, A.D. 6.

23.

C. I. L. iii. *Suppl.* 6687. This inscription was first noted in 1674. The
marble afterwards disappeared, and till recently the copy was regarded as a
forgery (cf. *C. I. L.* v. 136*) partly on account of the reference to the Census
of Quirinius in l. 9. In 1880 the lower part (printed below in capitals) was
discovered at Venice in the foundations of the house in which it was originally
said to have been preserved, and it is now admitted by Mommsen to be genuine
(*Eph. Epigr.* iv. p. 537). It came no doubt from Berytus, the only colony (l. 17)
in Syria in the time of Augustus with an appreciable Latin element, and there it
must have been that Secundus held the municipal offices of ll. 18, 19. l. 22 :
h(oc) m(onumentum) h(eredem) n(on) s(equitur).

Q. Aemilius Q. f.
Pal(atina) (tribu) Secundus, [in]
castris divi Aug. s[ub]
P. Sulpi[c]io Quirinio le[gato]
5 C[a]esaris Syriae honori-
bus decoratus, pr[a]efect(us)
cohort(is) Aug(ustae) I, pr[a]efect(us)
cohort(is) II classicae, IDEM
iussu Quirini CENSVM · EGI
10 ApamENAE · CIVITATIS · MIL
LIVM · HOMIN · CIVIVM · C̄X̄V̄Ī̄Ī̄
IDEM · MISSV · QVIRINI · ADVERSVS
ITVRAEOS · IN · LIBANO · MONTE ·
CASTELLVM · EORVM · CEPI · ET · ANTE
15 MILITIEM · PRAEFECT · FABRVM ·
DELATVS · A · DVOBVS · COS · AD · AE
RARIVM ET · IN · COLONIA ·
QVAESTOR · AEDIL · ĪĪ · DVVM VIR · ĪĪ
PONTIFEXS

20   IBI·POSITI·SVNT·Q·AEMILIVS·Q·F·PAL

       SECVNDVS·F·ET·AEMILIA·CHIA·LIB

       H · M · AMPLIVS · H · N · S ·

The events mentioned in ll. 9–14 took place during the
second tenure by Quirinius of the Governorship of Syria in
A.D. 6 (the first was in B.C. 3–2). The date is fixed by the
reference to the Census in Josephus, *Ant.* 18. 2 : τῶν ἀποτιμή-
σεων πέρας ἐχουσῶν αἳ ἐγένοντο τριακοστῷ καὶ ἑβδόμῳ ἔτει μετὰ
᾽Αντωνίου ἐν ᾽Ακτίῳ ἧτταν Καίσαρος. The Census in a province
was ordinarily carried out by officials of equestrian rank on
the governor's staff to whom special districts were assigned.
Hence it is probable that Secundus was holding one of the
praefecturae of ll. 6–8 when he took the Census at Apamea,
and the other will then belong to his expedition against the
Ityraei. Cf. *C. I. L.* xiv. 3955 = *D.* 2740 : *Gn. Munatius
M. f. Pal. Aurelius Bassus, proc(urator) Aug(usti), praef.
fabr., praef. coh. III sagittariorum, praef. coh. iterum II
Asturum, censitor civium Romanorum coloniae Victricensis
quae est in Brittannia Camaloduni, &c.* (*St. R.* ii. 1093). For
the Census in other provinces under Augustus, cf. the cases
of Gaul (Liv. *Ep.* 134, 136. Dio Cass. 53. 22. 5. Tac. *Ann.*
1. 31. 2), and Lusitania (*C. I. L.* x. 680 : [*ab imp.*] *Caesare
Aug.* [*missus pro*] *censore ad Lus*[*itanos*]).

The following points in the inscription may also be noticed.
The *honores* mentioned in l. 5 are the *equestres militiae* which
follow. Cf. *C. I. L.* ix. 3158 : . . . *usum castre(n)sibus Caesaris August(i) summis* [*eq*]*u*[*es*]*tris ordinis honoribus.* In
l. 7 the proper name of the cohort (regularly that of the
people among whom it was recruited) has been omitted.
The *praefecti fabrum* (l. 15) had lost their exclusively military
character by the time of Augustus, and are found on the
staff of the governor of an *inermis provincia* like Asia
(e. g. *C. I. L.* iii. *Suppl.* 7089, *praef. fabr.* to M'. Lepidus, Proconsul of Asia in A.D. 26, Tac. *Ann.* 4. 56. 3). For the
practice of outgoing Consuls and Praetors registering the

names of their *praefecti fabrum* at the Treasury, cf. Cic. *pro
Balb.* 28. 63: (*Caesar*) *in praetura, in consulatu, praefectum
fabrum detulit.* For the iteration (l. 16: *a duobus cos.*) cf.
C. I. L. iii. *Suppl.* 6983: *C. Iulius* [*Aquila pr*]*aef.· fabr. bis
in aerar. delatus a cos. A. Gabin*[*io Secundo, Ta*]*uro Statilio
Corvino.*

Mommsen, *Res Gestae Divi Aug.* 166, 175.   *C. I. L.* iii. *Suppl.* pp. 122, 3.

III. THE ORGANISATION OF ROME AND ITALY.

Rome.

24.

C. I. L. vi. 1244.   At Rome over the Porta S. Lorenzo, where the three
channels of the Aquae Marcia, Tepula, and Iulia (hence *aquarum omnium*, l. 4)
cross the road.   The date is B.C. 5-4.   Below this inscription records of
restorations of the Marcia by Titus in A. D. 79, and by Caracalla in A. D. 212
have been added.

IMP · CAESAR · DIVI · IVLI · F · AVGVSTVS
PONTIFEX · MAXIMVS · COS · XII
TRIBVNIC · POTESTAT · XIX · IMP · XIIII
RIVOS · AQVARVM · OMNIVM · REFECIT

Mon. Anc. 4. 10: rivos aquarum compluribus locis vetustate labentes refeci, et
aquam quae Marcia appellatur duplicavi fonte novo in rivum eius inmisso.

25.

C. I. L. vi. 1235*f.*   Found on the right bank of the Tiber near the Farnesina.
Censorinus and Gallus were Consuls in B. C. 8.   The expansion *r*(*ecto*) *r*(*igore*)
in l. 4 is made certain by a recently discovered cippus of Antoninus Pius on
which the words are written in full.   *Bull. Com.* xviii. (1890), 326.   Cp. Ulp.
Dig. 43. 15. 1. 5: *ripa ita recte definietur id quod flumen continet naturalem
rigorem cursus sui tenens.*

C · MARCIVS · L · F · CENSORINVS
C · ASINIVS · C · F · GALLVS
COS
EX · S · C · TERMIN · R · R · PROX · CIPP · P · XX
5   CVRATORES · RIPARVM · QVI · PRIMI · TERMINAVER
EX · S · C · RESTITVERVNT

G(aius) Marcius L. f. Censorinus, G(aius) Asinius C. f.
Gallus co(n)s(ules) ex s(enatus) c(onsulto) termin(averunt).
R(ecto) r(igore) prox(imus) cipp(us) p(edes) XX. Curatores
riparum qui primi terminaver(unt) ex s. c. restituerunt.

26.

C. I. L. vi. 1236 *a.* On a cippus of travertine, found in its original position
on the right bank of the Tiber opposite the Ripetta. Most of the examples
of this type also give the distance to the next stone as in the case of No. 25.
The seventeenth year of the *tribunicia potestas* of Augustus was from June 27th
B. C. 7 to June 26th B. C. 6.

IMP · CAESAR · DIVI · F

AVGVSTVS

PONTIFEX · MAXIMVS

TRIBVNIC · POTEST · $\overline{\text{XVII}}$

EX · S · C · TERMINAVIT

27.

C. I. L. ix. 3306. Found at Castelvecchio Subrego (Superaequum) and preserved there. Cf. Liebenam, *Legaten in den röm. Provinzen,* 397. *Quaesitor
iudex* was the title of the inferior class of presidents of the *quaestiones perpetuae,*
chosen from those who had not proceeded beyond the aedileship as opposed to
the *praetores quaesitores* (*St. R.* ii. 586. *W.* 1130, note 4).

Q · VÁRIO · Q · F ·
GEMINO ·
LEG · DIVI · AVG · $\overline{\text{II}}$ ·
PRO · COS · PR · TR · PL
5   Q · QVAESIT · IVDIC
PRAEF · FRVM · DAND
$\overline{\text{X}}$ · VIR · STL · IVDIC
CVRATORI · AEDIVM · SACR
MONVMENTOR · QVE · PVBLIC
10   TVENDORVM
IS · PRIMVS · OMNIVM · PAELIGN · SENATOR
FACTVS · EST · ET · EOS · HONORES · GESSIT
SVPERAEQVANI · PVBLICE
PATRONO

Q. Vario Q. f. Gemino, leg(ato) divi Aug(usti) II, proco(n)s(uli), pr(actori), tr(ibuno) pl(ebis), q(uaestori), quaesit(ori) iudic(i), praef(ecto) frum(enti) dand(i), X vir(o) stl(itibus) iudic(andis), curatori aedium sacr(arum) monumentor(um)que public(orum) tuendorum. Is primus omnium Paelign(orum) senator factus est et eos honores gessit. Superaequani publice patrono.

Mon. Anc. Gr. 3. 5 : οὐ παρητησάμην ἐν τῇ μεγίστῃ [τοῦ] σ[είτ]ου σπάνει τὴν ἐπιμέλειαν τῆς ἀγορᾶς, ἣν οὕ[τως ἐπετήδευ]σα, ὥστ᾽ ἐν ὀλίγαις ἡμέρα[ις το]ῦ παρόντος φόβου καὶ κι[νδ]ύνου ταῖς ἐμαῖς δαπάναις τὸν δῆμον ἐλευθερῶσα[ι].

The work of Augustus in providing for the material wants of the city of Rome, illustrated by Nos. 24–27, was only part of a great scheme for the regeneration of the capital of the Empire. Suetonius, *Aug.* 28 : *Urbem, neque pro maiestate imperii ornatam et inundationibus incendiisque obnoxiam, excoluit adeo, ut iure sit gloriatus, marmoream se relinquere, quam latericiam accepisset. Tutam vero, quantum provideri humana ratione potuit, etiam in posterum praestitit.* The important year for this policy was B.C. 8—the year of the third renewal of the Imperium of Augustus and of his second Census—when the regulation of the Tiber was taken in hand (Nos. 25, 26), and the organisation of Rome by *regiones* and *vici* was carried out (Dio Cass. 55. 8. 6). For the functions of the *magistri vicorum*, and the changes by which the arrangements for the preservation of order in the capital were put on a different basis which brought them immediately under the control of the Emperor (the *praefectura urbis* and *praefectura vigilum*) see p. 61. The results of this work of Augustus are to be judged not merely by the contrast between the ' Roma latericia ' and ' Roma marmorea,' but rather by that between the city of disorder and decay which he found (cf. *Mon. Anc.* 4. 17 : *duo et octoginta templa deum in urbe . . . refeci, nullo praetermisso quod e[o] temp[ore refici debebat]*), and the comparatively stately and well ordered capital which he left behind him.

Nos. 24–27 relate to three of the material reforms. (1) In

the matter of the water supply of Rome Augustus was rather a restorer than a creator (cf. with No. 24, *Mon. Anc.* 4. 10), and only two new aqueducts were erected under him, both by Agrippa; the Aqua Julia in B.C. 33 and the Virgo in B.C. 19. But the management of the supply, previously belonging to the Censors, was in B.C. 11 made over to the Emperor in constitutional form (Frontinus, *de Aq.* 99: *Q. Aelio Tuberone, Paulo Fabio Maximo consulibus, in re, quae usque in id tempus, quasi potestate acta, certo iure egerit, senatus consulta facta sunt ac lex promulgata*) as one of his personal charges (the *cura* is a *res ab Imperatore delegata*. Frontin. *de Aq.* ad init.) and placed on a permanent basis by the establishment of a board of *curatores* nominated by the Emperor (*ex consensu, ex auctoritate senatus* in the Senatus consulta of B.C. 11 in Frontin. 100, 104), and consisting of the head of the department and two assessors of inferior rank. Cf. Frontin. 99: [*Augustus*] *curatorem fecit Messallam Corvinum, cui adiutores dati Postumius Sulpicius praetorius et L. Cominius pedarius: insignia eis quasi magistratibus concessa, deque eorum officio senatus consultum factum.* Then follow the decrees, 100, 104, &c., &c.

(2) The regulation of the Tiber, conducted under the Republic by the Censors (the last *terminatio* before the time of Augustus was that of the Censors of B.C. 54 M. Valerius Messalla and P. Servilius Isauricus, *C. I. L.* vi. 1234), fell to the Emperor as general inheritor of the Censorial power. For the necessity of a special department cf. Hor. 1 *C. 2. 13.* Suet. *Aug.* 28: *Urbem ... inundationibus ... obnoxiam*, and 30: *ad coercendas inundationes alveum Tiberis laxavit ac repurgavit, completum olim ruderibus et aedificiorum prolationibus coartatum.* Though Suetonius mentions the Tiber among the *curae* organised by Augustus (37: *nova officia excogitavit: curam ... alvei Tiberis*), it is clear from Nos. 25, 26, that the *terminatio* of B.C. 8–7 was begun by the Consuls and finished by Augustus himself. Apparently the Consuls had dealt with the course of the river in the centre and southern part of the city, leaving

only the region of the Campus Martius to be finished by
the Emperor. Six out of the nine cippi of Augustus in *C. I. L.*
vi. 1236 *a–i* were found in or near the Castle of St. Angelo.
The source of the other three is not known. The recent
discovery in the same region of thirteen more ' in situ ' has
thrown considerable light on the way in which the *terminatio*
was carried out (see D. Marchetti in the *Notizie degli Scavi,*
1890, 32, &c., *Bull. Com.* xx. (1892), 71). It was not until the
floods of A. D. 15 (Dio Cass. 57. 14. 7. Tac. *Ann.* 1. 76) that a
permanent board of five *curatores* was established by Tiberius
(No. 25. 5); Dio Cass. 57. 14. 8 : πέντε ἀεὶ βουλευτὰς κληρωτοὺς
ἐπιμελεῖσθαι τοῦ ποταμοῦ προσέταξεν. Tacitus l. c. says that the
immediate measures of relief were entrusted to Ateius Capito
and L. Arruntius. We know from the list in Frontinus (*de Aq.*
102) that at this time Capito was *curator aquarum,* and it is
possible that the existing *curatores aquarum* may at first have
co-operated with the new board of which L. Arruntius would
be the president (*C. I. L.* vi. p. 266). The *curatores* acted, like
the Censors and Augustus, *ex senatus consulto.* Under Claudius
the formula *ex auctoritate* (*Imperatoris*) first appears (*Bull. Com.*
xv. (1887), 306), and from Vespasian onwards it is regular
(*C. I. L.* vi. 1238 sqq.).

(3) In order that the public buildings of the city of Rome
and especially the temples, should not again fall into the
condition in which he found them (cf. *Mon. Anc.* 4. 17 quoted
above), Augustus provided for the continuance of the old
Censorial functions in this and analogous spheres (Livy, 42. 3.
7 : *censorem . . . cui sarta tecta exigere sacris publicis et loca
tuenda more maiorum traditum esset*) by the appointment of
two *curatores.* Their title appears in various forms (perhaps
curator aedium sacrarum locorum et operum publicorum was
the full expression), and later was often shortened into *curatores operum publicorum.* The date of their institution is
uncertain, and Q. Varius Geminus, the earliest *curator* that
we know of (No. 27), may belong as well to the beginning of

the principate of Tiberius as to the end of that of Augustus. However Suetonius (*Aug.* 37) mentions the *cura operum publicorum* among the other departments which (with the exception of that of the Tiber) we know were created by Augustus. The *curatores* were entrusted not only with the maintenance of public buildings and the custody of their contents (cf. Suet. *Vitellius,* 5 : *in urbano officio* [i. e. the *cura operum publicorum*] *dona atque ornamenta templorum subripuisse et commutasse quaedam ferebatur*), but also with the power of leasing land in the city belonging to the State. Transactions of this kind are illustrated by the documents given in *C. I. L.* vi. 1585= *D.* 5920 (A.D. 193), which relate to the granting of a site for a private building subject to a ground rent (*solarium*).

For the series of new buildings erected by Augustus, see *Mon. Anc.* 4. 1–23.

The office of *praefectus frumenti dandi* held by Q. Varius Geminus (No. 27. 6), must not be confused with the Imperial department which regulated the food supply of the capital (*cura annonae,* cf. *Mon. Anc.* Gr. 3. 5), perhaps the most important of the ways by which the Emperor kept a firm grasp over the city, and at the same time made himself indispensable to it. The confusion is possible because the members of the board of quasi-magistrates established in B.C. 22–18 for this purpose (chosen by lot from Senators of the first class) were called *praefecti frumenti dandi* as well as *curatores frumenti* (both occur in the same Senatus consultum of B.C. 11 in Frontin. *de Aq.* 100, 101). Before the death of Augustus the department had been brought under the Emperor's immediate control with a permanent official of the equestrian order at its head (the earliest *praefectus annonae* that we know of is C. Turranius in A.D. 14 ; Tac. *Ann.* 1. 7. 3). But *praefecti frumenti dandi,* generally with the addition *ex senatus consulto,* continue to occur. They are of inferior standing (often *aedilicii*) to the old *praefecti,* and were probably called into existence to carry out exceptional distributions at the expense of the

Aerarium.   Q. Varius Geminus must have been one of these.
No inscriptions of the old *praefecti-curatores* are known (*St. R.*
ii. 1041, note 1).

Hirschfeld, *Verwaltungsbeamten*, pp. 273, 262, 265, 230.

Italy.

28.

C. I. L. v. 2501.   Epitaph from the territory of Ateste (Este).

<pre>
        M · BILLIENVS · M · F
        ROM   ·   ACTIACVS
        LEGIONE · X̄Ī · PROE
        LIO · NAVALI · FACTO
  5   INCOLONIAM . DE
        DVCTVS · AB · ORDI
        NE · DECVRIO · ALLEC
</pre>

*M. Billienus M. f. Rom(ilia) (tribu), Actiacus, legione XI,
proelio navali facto in coloniam deductus, ab ordine decurio
allec[tus ......*

Mon. Anc. 5. 36 : Italia autem XXVIII [colo]nias, quae vivo me celeberrimae
et frequentissimae fuerunt, me[is auspicis] deductas habet.

29.

C. I. L. xi. 365.   On the triumphal arch at Rimini (Ariminum) crossing the
Via Flaminia.   The date is B.C. 27.

SENATVS · POPVLVSQ*ue romanus*
imp. caesari diui f. augusto imp. sept
COS · SEPT · DESIGNAT · OCTAVOM · *Via flami-
n*IA *et reliquei*S
CELEBERRIMEIS · ITALIAE · VIEIS · CONSILIO
*et sumptib*VS *eius mu*NITEIS

Mon. Anc. 4. 19 : con[s]ul septimum viam Flaminiam a[b urbe] Ari[minum
feci].

30.

B. M. C. Emp. i, Aug. 79.   Cf. Eckhel, vi. 105.   Denarius of B.C. 17–16.

Obverse.   AVGVSTVS TR. POT. VII.   Head of Augustus.

Reverse.   L. VINICIVS L. F. III VIR round a cippus on which

is inscribed S. P. Q. R. IMP. CAE(*sari*) QVOD V(*iae*)
M(*unitae*) S(*unt*) EX EA P(*ecunia*) Q(*uam*) IS AD A(*era-
rium*) DE(*tulit*).

Italy at the beginning of the Principate called for the
attention of Augustus not less than the city of Rome. Not
to speak of the centres of disaffection in some of the towns
(Dio Cass. 51. 4. 6 : δήμους τοὺς ἐν τῇ Ἰταλίᾳ τοὺς τὰ τοῦ Ἀντωνίου
φρονήσαντας), there were districts in which public security
had practically disappeared. Suet. *Aug.* 32 : *grassatorum
plurimi palam se ferebant succincti ferro, quasi tuendi sui
causa, et rapti per agros viatores sine discrimine liberi servique
ergastulis possessorum supprimebantur . . . Igitur grassaturas
dispositis per opportuna loca stationibus inhibuit, ergastula
recognovit.* Cf. Dio Cass. 49. 43. 5. Above all the political
and economic disorders of the period which began with the
Social War and the confiscations of Sulla had fatally affected
the prosperity of the country. These inscriptions relate to
two ways in which Augustus attempted to infuse new life
into Italy, and at the same time to consolidate his position
and to make his influence felt.

(1) The 28 colonies founded by Augustus in Italy (*Mon.
Anc.* 5. 36) cannot all be identified with certainty, partly because we do not know how many of those founded during the
Triumvirate (B.C. 43–27) were regarded by him as of his own
creation and reckoned with those founded after the battle
of Actium (*Mon. Anc.* 3. 22), partly because we cannot feel
sure that he excluded his three colonies in Illyricum (Iader,
Salonae, Narona. Illyricum at least, is omitted from the list
of provinces in which he founded colonies, *Mon. Anc.* 5. 35.)
But if we accept the list of Mommsen (*Res Gest. D. Aug.*
123 : for the evidence see *Hermes,* xviii. 161), putting aside
four in Etruria (Castrum Novum, Pisae, Saena, Sutrium) and
one in Picenum (Falerio), it will be seen that geographically the colonies fall into three groups; those in the part of

Italy previously known as Cisalpine Gaul (Ateste, Augusta Praetoria, Augusta Taurinorum, Bononia, Brixia, Concordia, Dertona, Parentium, Parma, Pola), those along or near the line of the Via Flaminia (Ariminum, Fanum Fortunae, Hispellum, Lucus Feroniae, Pisaurum, Tuder, and to these we might perhaps add Sutrium), and those in Campania and the neighbouring parts (Abellinum, Beneventum, Capua, Minturnae, Nola, Sora, Suessa, Venafrum). By this arrangement Augustus secured (1) centres of loyalty to himself and the Empire, placed in the most prosperous and influential districts of Italy (N.B. the exclusion of *Apulia . . . inanissima pars Italiae,* Cicero *ad Att.* 8. 3. 4), and ready if necessary to give a more than sentimental support to his government; (2) a series of permanent garrisons for securing communications by the road which was ' par excellence' the Emperor's highway to the armies of the Rhine and the Danube, and the provinces which they covered (Dio Cass. 53. 22 quoted below). There was probably a further thought for the protection of Italy by the foundation of towns to guard its eastern and western gates. Notice e. g. the position of Augusta Praetoria, Augusta Taurinorum, Concordia, Ateste, and cf. that of Bononia at the point where all the main roads to Rome converge.

The colonies in some cases replaced transported communities (Dio Cass. 51. 4. 6 : τοὺς γὰρ δήμους τοὺς ἐν τῇ 'Ιταλίᾳ τοὺς τὰ τοῦ 'Αντωνίου φρονήσαντας ἐξοικίσας τοῖς μὲν στρατιώταις τάς τε πόλεις καὶ τὰ χωρία αὐτῶν ἐχαρίσατο), in others introduced a new element into existing ones (as at Ateste). In considering the effect which they were intended to produce on the prosperity of Italy, it must not be forgotten that the colonists brought a considerable amount of capital into the towns in which they settled (*Mon. Anc.* 3. 17 : *in colon[i]s militum meorum consul quintum ex manibiis viritim millia nummum singula dedi; acceperunt id triumphale congiarium in colo-[n]is hominum circiter centum et viginti millia*). That a real effect was produced may be inferred from the increase of

population under Augustus. In B.C. 28 the returns of the
Census gave 4,063,000 as the number of Roman citizens,
in B.C. 8, 4,233,000, in A.D. 14, 4,937,000 (*Mon. Anc.* 2. 4,
2. 6, 2. 10).

(2) No. 29 is a monument of the completion by Augustus
in B.C. 27 (and therefore the earliest of his reforms in home
administration) of the repair of the roads of Italy. The distinction between the Via Flaminia and the other roads which
he made on that occasion (Dio Cass. 53. 22 : τὰς μὲν ἄλλας
[ὁδοὺς] ἄλλοις τισὶ τῶν βουλευτῶν ἐπισκευάσαι τοῖς οἰκείοις τέλεσι
προσέταξε, τῆς δὲ δὴ Φλαμινίας αὐτός, ἐπειδήπερ ἐκστρατεύσειν δι'
αὐτῆς ἤμελλεν, ἐπεμελήθη) is suggestive of the two reasons
which made the *cura viarum* an important element in the
administration of Italy and the Empire. On the one hand
the Via Flaminia was the great means of communication by
land between Rome and the Empire, and not the least important of the creations of Augustus was the Imperial despatch
service which must have largely used this road (Suet. *Aug.* 49).
On the other hand the *curatores* of that and the other roads in
Italy, who in B.C. 20 replaced the temporary commissioners
of B.C. 27, through the local jurisdiction which they exercised
took no small share in the government of the country. The
cura was constitutionally transferred to the Emperor (Dio
Cass. 54. 8. 4 (B.C. 20): τότε δὲ αὐτός τε προστάτης τῶν περὶ
τὴν Ῥώμην ὁδῶν αἱρεθείς. Cf. the case of the *cura aquarum.*
Probably all the *curae* were established in the same manner
St. R. ii. 1044), who then appointed a *curator* for each of the
great roads (Dio Cass. l. c.). The funds for the department
were paid through the Aerarium, but were provided to a large
extent by the Emperor himself (Statius, *Silv.* 3. 3. 102, mentions the *longe series porrecta viarum* as one of the regular
expenses of the Fiscus). A special liberality of this kind in
B.C. 16 was commemorated by No. 30. There are similar
coins of the next year (*B.M.C. Emp.* i, Aug. 80 : *tr. pot. VIII*).

The Frontier of Italy. Conquest of the Alps, B.C. 16-14.

31.

C. I. L. v. 7817. Plinius, *H. N.* 3. 136: *non alienum videtur hoc loco subicere inscriptionem e Tropaeo Alpium quae talis est* (then follows, No. 31). We have here an instance of an inscription depending mainly on a copy, but a copy which goes back to classical times. The Tropaeum Alpium, the form of which was perhaps suggested by the Tropaea Pompeii (Plin. *H. N.* 3. 18: *cum Pompeius Magnus tropaeis suis quae statuebat in Pyrenaeo, DCCCLXXVII oppida ab Alpibus ad fines Hispaniae ulterioris in dicionem a se redacta testatus sit.* 37. 15: *nonne illa similior tui est imago quam Pyrenaei iugis imposuisti?*), to judge by the description of the remains which still existed in the sixteenth century (*C.I.L.* v. p. 904) was a circular structure on a square base crowned by a statue of Augustus (the ἁψὶς τροπαιοφόρος of Dio Cass. 53. 26. 5 is therefore different, and perhaps refers to the existing arch at Aosta. *C. I. L.* v. p. 907). It stood on the seaward face of the Maritime Alps above Monoecus (Monaco) and gave its name to the place, whence the modern Turbia, where unimportant fragments of the inscription have been found which are now in the Museum of St. Germain. One corrects *Triumpilini* of the MSS.

Imp. Caesari divi f. Augusto pontifici
maxumo imp. XIIII tribunic. potestate XVII S. P. Q. R.
quod eius ductu auspicisque gentes Alpinae omnes quae
a mari supero ad inferum pertinebant sub imperium p. R. sunt redactae.

gentes alpinae devictae	Focunates	Rugusci	Varagri	Brodionti	Vergunni
Trumpilini	Vindelicorum gentes	Suanetes	Salassi	Nemaloni	Egui
Camunni	quattuor	Calucones	Acitavones	Edenates	Turi
Venostes	Cosuanetes	Brixenetes	Medulli	Esubiani	Nematuri
Vennonetes	Rucinates	Leponti	Ucenni	Veamini	Oratelli
Isarci	Licates	Uberi	Caturiges	Gallitae	Nerusi
Breuni	Catenates	Nantuates	Brigiani	Triullatti	Velauni
Genaunes	Ambisontes	Seduni	Sogionti	Ecdini	Suetri

32.

C. I. L. v. 7231. Repeated on both faces of the triumphal arch at Susa (Segusio). After giving the inscription of the Tropaea Alpium, Plinius continues (*H. N.* 3. 138): *non sunt adiectae Cottianae civitates XV quae non fuerunt hostiles.* Only fourteen appear here, and of these, six are included in the list of the Tropaea (Edenates = Adanates. Esubiani = Vesubiani). The date is B. C. 9–8.

IMP · CAESARI · AVGVSTO · DIVI · F · PONTIFICI ·
MAXVMO · TRIBVNIC · POTESTATE · XV · IMP · XIII |
M · IVLIVS · REGIS · DONNI · F · COTTIVS · PRAEFECTVS ·
CEIVITATIVM · QVAE · SVBSCRIPTAE · SVNT · SEGOVIORVM ·
SEGVSINORVM · | BELACORVM · CATVRIGVM · MEDVLLORVM ·
TEBAVIORVM · ADANATIVM · SAVINCATIVM · ECDINIORVM ·
VEAMINIORVM | VENISAMORVM · IEMERIORVM · VESVBIANI-
ORVM · QVADIATIVM · ET · CEIVITATES · QVAE · SVB · EO ·
PRAEFECTO · FVERVNT

Mon. Anc. 5. 12 : [Alpes a re]gione ea, quae proxima est Hadriano mari, [ad Tuscum pacari fec]i nulli genti bello per iniuriam inlato.

The conquest of the Alpine region (cf. *Mon. Anc.* 5. 12 and No. 31. 4) together with Raetia and Noricum, took place between B. C. 16–14, the Salassi having been reduced as early as B. C. 25 (Dio Cass. 53. 25. 3). The decisive series of operations was the combined attack in B. C. 15 by Drusus from the side of Italy advancing through the Brenner Pass (No. 33), and Tiberius from the side of Gaul, the culminating success being the victory of the latter at the lake of Constance, and the final result the pushing forward of the frontier to the upper waters of the Danube (Dio Cass. 54. 22. 3. Vell. Pat. 2. 95. Hor. 4 *C.* 14. For the minor operations of B. C. 16 and 14, see Dio Cass. 54. 20, 24. 3). We may suppose that it was after the completion of the new organisation of the districts that the Tropaeum Alpium was erected in B. C. 7–6. The arch of Segusio was finished more than a year before.

These acquisitions were important for two reasons. In the first place the fertile land between the Padus and the Alps was secured from the raids of the mountain tribes. For the previous state of things cf. Hirt. *B. G.* 8. 24: *legionem autem XV ... in togatam Galliam mittit ad colonias civium Romanorum tuendas ne quod simile incommodum accideret decursione barbarorum ac superiore aestate Tergestinis acciderat, qui repentino latrocinio atque impetu eorum erant oppressi.* Plin. *H. N.* 18. 182: *Salassi cum subiectos Alpibus depopularentur agros.* Dio Cass. 54. 22: [B.C. 15] 'Ραιτοὶ ... ἐκ τῆς 'Ιταλίας ἁρπαγὰς ἐποιοῦντο. Hence no doubt the justification of Augustus in *Mon. Anc.* 5. 14: *nulli genti bello per iniuriam inlato.* Secondly, it was essential that the communications between Italy and the provinces both eastern and western should be in Roman hands. The direct road, e.g. to Lugudunum passed through the Salassi: hence perhaps the early settlement of this part of the question, and the foundation of the veteran colony of Augusta Praetoria (Dio Cass. 53. 25. 5).

These sub-Alpine districts illustrate the ways in which Rome dealt with subject peoples when it was not possible or advisable to include them in a province of the ordinary type.

(1) The policy of attaching native communities (*gentes, civitates, oppida*) as subjects to Roman towns in their neighbourhood (*attribuere, contribuere*), dating in this district from the times of the Republic (Plin. *H. N.* 3. 138: in the list of the Tropaea are not included the communities *attributae municipiis lege Pompeia* [B.C. 89], cf. Tac. *Hist.* 3. 34. 2: [Cremona founded B.C. 218] *adnexu conubiisque gentium adolevit floruitque*), was now extended to the newly conquered tribes in the central and eastern part of the southern slope of the Alps. Thus the Bergalei were 'attributed' to Comum (see No. 79. 10); the Trumpilini, Benacenses, Camunni, Sabini to Brixia (Plin. *H. N.* 3. 134. *C. I. L.* v. pp. 512, 515); the Anauni, Tulliasses, Sinduni, to Tridentum (see No. 79. 23); the Carni and Catali to Tergeste (*C. I. L.* v. 532. 2. 3 = D. 6680: *Carni Catalique attributi a divo Augusto rei publicae*

nostrae). These communities retain a distinct existence (hence
they occasionally appear as the domiciles of legionaries coming
from them. *C. I. L.* iii. Suppl. 7452 epitaph of *L. Plinius
Sex. f. Fab(ia) (tribu) domo Trumplia mil(es) leg(ionis) XX
&c.*), but they have no civil organisation of their own (there
are only traces of the native headman. *C. I. L.* v. 4910 :
princeps Trumplinorum, 4893 : *princeps Sabinorum*) and are
governed by the town magistrates. The intention of this
arrangement was primarily to provide for the government of
the tribes, but ultimately to raise them by force of contact
to the level of the governing community, so that they might
be admitted to share the full rights of citizenship with it.
(Originally they are of inferior political status, Plin. *H. N.*
3. 133 : *Latini iuris Euganeae gentes* [among them the
Trumpilini and Camunni]. The Carni and Catali were
apparently *iuris peregrini* before the *ius Latinum* was given
by Antoninus Pius, *C. I. L.* v. 532). Cf. No. 79 for the
development in the case of the Anauni.

(2) The western Alps were treated on a different principle.
Here, whether in view of stronger national unions among the
native communities, or that for other reasons the danger to
peace was greater, a system of centralisation under military
commanders was adopted. The tribes were formed by groups
into governmental districts, which were placed under officials
of equestrian rank appointed by the Emperor. Thus the
Alpes Maritimae was governed by a *praefectus*. One occurs
in No. 90 : *praefectus civitatium in Alpibus Maritumis,* and
may be compared with the *praefectus civitatium Moesiae et
Treballiae* of the same inscription, the analogous *praefectus
gentis Musulamiorum (C. I. L.* viii. 5351), *praefectus gentis
Cinithiorum (C. I. L.* viii. 10500), *ex praefecto gentis Masat
. . . (C. I. L.* viii. 9195) in Africa, and Tac. *Ann.* 4. 72. 2 :
Olennius e primipilaribus regendis Frisiis inpositus. Cf. p. 115.
This method of governing districts, which for special reasons
were left outside the regular system of provincial administration,

was an extension of the practice at the end of the Republic by which the governor sent *praefecti* to administer outlying portions of the province (Cic. *ad Att.* 5. 21. 6: *Q. Volusium ... misi in Cyprum ut ibi pauculos dies esset, ne cives Romani pauci qui illic negotiantur ius sibi dictum negarent; nam evocari ex insula Cyprios non licet*). By A.D. 69 thè *praefectus* had been replaced by a *procurator* (Tac. *Hist.* 2. 12. 5). The change, though mainly one of name (*nomine magis mutato quam rerum forma*, Mommsen in *C. I. L.* v. p. 902), may have been partly due to an increase in the fiscal importance of the district consequent on its advance in civilisation (cf. Tac. *Ann.* 15. 32: *eodem anno* [A.D. 63] *Caesar nationes Alpium Maritimarum in ius Latii transtulit*). For the military force under the *praefectus* and *procurator* cf. Tac. *Hist.* 2. 14. 3 : *Ligurum cohors vetus loci auxilium.* Several epitaphs of soldiers of the *cohors I Ligurum* have come from Cemenelum, the chief place in the Maritime Alps (*C. I. L.* v. p. 903). For the local militia see Tac. *Hist.* 2. 12. 5.

The Alpes Cottiae, where a national union of the tribes had existed from pre-Roman times (Regnum Cottii), were also governed by a *praefectus*, but here the native dynasty was made use of, the princes of the house of Cottius appearing as the *praefecti* appointed by the Emperor (No. 32), an arrangement which is explained by Pliny *H. N.* 3. 138 (quoted above). Under Claudius they even recovered their old title and independence (Dio Cass. 60. 24. 4), but on the extinction of the line Nero restored the province (Suet. *Nero*, 18).

O. Hirschfeld, *Die ritterlichen Provinzialstatthalter : Sitzungsberichte der k. pr. Akademie der Wissenschaften zu Berlin*, 1889, 425 sqq.

Raetia and Noricum. The Via Claudia Augusta.

33.

C. I. L. v. 8002. Milestone belonging to the restoration by Claudius in A. D. 47 of the Via Claudia Augusta (previously Via Augusta) originally made by the elder Drusus after the conquest of Raetia in B. C. 15. Found near Feltre (Feltria), so that the road probably joined that coming direct from Verona up the valley of the Adige at Tridentum. One other stone has been found near Meran (*C. I. L.* v. 8003), containing the variant *a flumine Pado ad flumen Danuvium.* No milestones of the original Via Augusta have been discovered. For the form .L in l. 11 cf. No. 9.

TI · CLAVDIVS · DRVSI · F

CAESAR · AVG · GERMA

NICVS · PONTIFEX · MAXV

MVS · TRIBVNICIA · POTESTA

5   TE · VI̅ · COS · IV̅ · IMP · XI · P · P

CENSOR · VIAM · CLAVDIAM

AVGVSTAM · QVAM · DRVSVS

PATER · ALPIBVS · BELLO · PATE

FACTIS · DEREX*e*RAT · MVNIT · AB

10   ALTINO · VSQVE · AD · FLVMEN

DANVVIVM · M · P · CCCL

In B.C. 42 Gallia Cisalpina, with its governor and his army, disappeared from the list of provinces. In order therefore that Italy should not be at once the centre of the Empire and yet a part of its frontier, the provinces of Raetia and Noricum were created between the Alps and the Danube which thus became the frontier of the Empire (No. 33. 10). For the conquest see p. 37. The same reasons which had caused the removal of the Proconsul and his army from Cisalpine Gaul, made it unadvisable to create a province of the first rank here, and therefore governors essentially of the same class as those of the western Alps (*procuratores*), the difference being one of degree and not of kind, were placed in charge of the two districts and of the troops which defended them. These were of the second class, supplemented by the local militia. Tac. *Hist.* 1. 68. 2 : *Raeticae alae cohortesque et ipsorum Raetorum iuventus sueta armis et more militiae exercita* (cf. p. 40 of the Maritime Alps). But in the course of the second century political reasons had to give way to the necessities of the Empire, and the pressure of the barbarians on the Upper Danube was met by transferring each province to a *legatus pro praetore* with a legion under his command.

The Via Claudia Augusta was important as being the means of communication with the frontier garrisons on the Danube, and also with Augusta Vindelicorum (Augsburg), the chief Roman centre in Raetia (Tac. *Germ.* 41 : *in splendidissima Raetiae provinciae colonia.* Probably as old as the time of Augustus, but only a *caput gentis* and not a *municipium*, till Hadrian).

IV. THE IMPERIAL FAMILY.

The arch of Ticinum (No. 34) is the earliest monument in which the idea of a Roman Imperial family can be traced. We are still far from the days of the 'domus divina' (hardly ever mentioned before the third century), but the appearance of the wife of the Princeps on a public monument marks a new departure, even though she is only called *uxor Caesaris Augusti*, and has as yet no official titles of her own (Agrippina, wife of Claudius, was the first to be called Augusta in the lifetime of her husband : *mater castrorum*, &c., not before Severus). As Augustus had no direct male descendants, it is an Imperial family produced by a process of selection, and, with one exception (10, the future Emperor Claudius), only those living persons are admitted to a place on this monument who can trace their connection, by adoption or otherwise, with the Emperor's adopted son Tiberius. This is important as establishing a line of succession to the Principate, for, however true it may be that the Constitution of the Principate contained no provision for a regular succession, the position of Tiberius as Heir Apparent is marked out quite as much by the fact that he is the adopted son of the Princeps as by his possession of the *imperium* and *tribunicia potestas* (cf. Tac. *Ann.* 1. 3. 3 : *illuc cuncta vergere : filius, collega imperii, consors tribuniciae potestatis adsumitur.* So in *Hist.* 1. 14 the adoption of Piso by Galba is spoken of as

. [*nisi necessa*]rii hominis erit eique spectaculis publicis eius
[*provinciae loco* . . . *interesse liceto*].

De honoribus eius qui flamen f[*uerit*].

10 [*Si qui flamen fue*]rit adversus hanc legem nihil fecerit, tum is
qui flamen erit c[*urato per duoviros ut* . . .]

[*per tabell*]as iurati decernant placeatne ei qui flamonio
abierit permitti sta[*tuam sibi ponere. Cui ita de-
creverint*]

[*ius esse sta*]tuae ponendae nomenque suum patrisque et
unde sit et quo anno fla[*men fuerit inscribendi, ei*]

[*Narbo*]ne intra fines eius templi statuae ponendae ius
esto, nisi cui imperator [*Caesar Augustus inter-
dixerit. Eidem*]

[*i*]n curia sua et concilio provinciae Narbonesis inter sui
ordinis secundum le[*gem*] . . . .

15 sententiae dicendae signandique ius esto, item spectaculo
publico in provincia [*edendo inter decuriones interesse prae-*]

textato eisque diebus, quibus, cum flamen esset, sacrificium
fecerit, ea veste pu[*blice uti, qua in eo faciendo usus
est*].

Si flamen in civitate esse des[*ierit*].

Si flamen in civitate esse desierit, neque ei subrogatus erit,
tum uti quis[*que flamen coloniae* (?) *Narbone erit*]

in triduo, quo certior factus erit et poterit, Narbon[*e*]
sacra facito [*omniaque secundum hanc legem per
reliquam*]

20 partem eius anni eo ordine habeto, quo annuorum flami-
n[*um habentur eique si ea fecerit per dies non
minus*]

XXX, siremps lex ius causaque esto, quae flamini Augus[*tali ex hac lege facto erit*].

Quo loco conciliu[*m provinciae habendum sit*].

Qui in concilium provinciae convenerint N[*arbonem, ibi id
habento. Si quid extra Narbonem finesve Narbone-*]

sium concilio habito actum erit, id ius rat[*umque ne esto*].

25   De pecu[*nia sacris destinata*].

Qui flamonio abierit, is ex ea pecunia, [*quae sacris destinata
     erit, quod eius superfuerit, statu-*]

as imaginesve imperatoris Caes[*aris Augusti* . . . . .
     arbitratu eius qui eo anno pro-]

vinciae praeerit intra idem t[*emplum dedicaro* . . *seque
     omnia sic ut hac lege cautum est de*]

ea re, fecisse apud eum qui ra[*tiones provinciae putabit
     probato*] . . . . .

36.

Allmer, *Lyon*, ii. p. 87.   De Boissieu, *Inscriptions de Lyon*, p. 278.   Found at
Lyons and now in the Museum there.

```
        TIB   •   POMPÉIO
      POMPEI • IV́STI • FÍL
      PRÍSCO   •   CADVR
      CO • OMNIBVS • HO
  5   NORƁ • APVD • SVÓS
      FV́NCT • TRIB • LEG • V
      MACEDONICAE
      IV́DICI   •   ARCAE
      GALLIÁRVM • ĪĪĪ
  10  PRÓVN̄C   •   GALLIÁE
```

37.

C. I. L. ii. 4248.   On the base of a statue at Tarraco where it was found.
Bergidum Flavium mentioned in l. 2 was probably between Asturica and Lucus
Augusti.   It was no doubt founded by Vespasian.

```
      C   •  VAL  •   ARABINO
      FLAVIANI • F • BERGƊO • F
      OMNIB • HON • IN RE • P
      SVA • FVNC • SACERDOTI
  5   ROMAE • ET • AVG • P • H • C
      OB • CVRAM • TABVLARI
```

```
        CENSVALIS   FIDELITER
        ADMINISTR  ·  STATVAM
        INTER  ·  FLAMINALES
10      VIROS  ·  POSITAM  ·  EX
        ORNANDVM  .  VNIVERS
        CENSVER
```

C. Val(erio) Arabino Flaviani f., Bergido f(laviensi), omnib(us) hon(oribus) in re p(ublica) sua func(to), sacerdoti Romae et Aug(usti), p(rovincia) H(ispania) c(iterior); ob curam tabulari censualis fideliter administr(atam) statuam inter flaminales viros exornand[a]m univers(i) censuer(unt).

No. 35 is the only document of any length that we possess relating to the Concilia with their presidents the priests of Augustus, which were organised in every province for the worship of the Emperor. Although this is a special statute for Gallia Narbonensis, it may be regarded as typical of the form taken in the West by an institution which was common to the whole Empire. Everywhere the political reason for its existence was applicable, viz. the necessity of creating in a State which had neither monarchical traditions nor national unity, a feeling of loyalty to the Emperor, and a sense of membership in the Empire. Everywhere too we find the same fundamental organisation, viz. an assembly of deputies (σύνεδροι, *legati*) elected by the communities of the province meeting annually at a central temple of Rome and Augustus under the presidency of an elected high-priest (ἀρχιερεύς, *sacerdos, flamen provinciae*). But the starting-point for the system was found in the Hellenised East, which was familiar with the worship of Alexander and his successors, and where in Republican times the Greek cities had been accustomed to erect temples not only to the city of Rome, as Smyrna had done so early as B.C. 195 (Tac. *Ann.* 4. 56), but also to Roman generals and governors (Plut. *Flamininus*, 16: at Chalcis ἔτι δὲ καὶ καθ' ἡμᾶς ἱερεὺς χειροτονητὸς ἀπεδείκνυτο Τίτου.

Cf. Cic. *ad Q. f.* 1. 1. 9. 26). It was quite natural therefore that the object of the new State-cult should be defined as *Roma et Augustus* (Suet. *Aug.* 52 : *templa, quamvis sciret etiam proconsulibus decerni solere, in nulla tamen provincia nisi communi suo Romaeque nomine recepit*). As it was important that the worship should be general, an organisation was wanted which should unite all the communities of a province in its practice. Here again it was in the Greek part of the Empire that the principle of such an organisation was found, for several of the old national representative congresses (κοινά, συνέδρια) survived the Roman Conquest ; and though it is not clear how far, if at all, there was in any case actual continuity between them and the Imperial assemblies, they certainly provided the pattern on which the latter were modelled. (Pausanias, 7. 16. 10 : ἐτράποντο ἐς ἔλεον Ῥωμαῖοι τῆς Ἑλλάδος καὶ συνέδρια κατὰ ἔθνος ἀποδιδόασιν ἑκάστοις τὰ ἀρχαῖα. For the federal assembly of Lycia under Augustus see Strabo, 14. 3. 2, p. 664 ; *commune Siciliae*, Cic. *Verr.* 2. 2. 46. 114 ; κοινὸν τῶν Ἀχαιῶν, Mommsen, *Prov.* i. 264. Asia on the other hand probably never had a κοινόν before Augustus. Waddington, iii. p. 245.) The system was inaugurated in Asia and Bithynia in B.C. 29. Dio Cass. 51. 20. 7 : τοῖς δὲ δὴ ξένοις, Ἕλληνάς σφας ἐπικαλέσας, ἑαυτῷ τινα, τοῖς μὲν Ἀσιανοῖς ἐν Περγάμῳ τοῖς δὲ Βιθυνοῖς ἐν Νικομηδείᾳ, τεμενίσαι ἐπέτρεψε. καὶ τοῦτ' ἐκεῖθεν ἀρξάμενον καὶ ἐπ' ἄλλων αὐτοκρατόρων οὐ μόνον ἐν τοῖς Ἑλληνικοῖς ἔθνεσιν, ἀλλὰ καὶ ἐν τοῖς ἄλλοις ὅσα τῶν Ῥωμαίων ἀκούει, ἐγένετο. The earliest evidence for the Concilium in Asia is the coin of B.C. 19, with *Com(mune) As(iae) Rom(ae) et August(o)* (*B.M.C. Emp.* i, Aug. 705. Eckhel, vi. 100). In every province, including those which were added to the Empire at a later date (e.g. Britain, Tac. *Ann.* 14. 31. 6, and Dacia), this pattern was reproduced. In the West the earliest certain case is the altar to Rome and Augustus dedicated in B.C. 12 at Lugudunum as a centre for the Three Gauls (Nos. 16, 17) and here, as in the East, the new institution seems to have been adapted to a pre-existing national institution, for Aug. 1, the day of the dedication of the altar (Suet. *Cl.* 2) and of the meeting of the Concilium, was also the great Celtic festival of the Sun-god Lug (Prof. Rhŷs, *Hibbert Lectures*, 409, 421, 424). We know nothing about the date of the foundation of the altar or temple with its Concilium for Narbonensis, but it must belong to the time of Augustus. When Germany was lost in A.D. 9 an altar had been set up at the *oppidum Ubiorum* (Köln) as a centre for the province, just as the altar at Lugudunum was a centre for the Gauls (Tac. *Ann.* 1. 57. 2). At Tarraco, where an altar had existed under Augustus, a temple was erected in A.D. 15 (Tac. *Ann.* 4. 37). Finally we learn from *C. I. L.* iii. 2810 = *D.* 7157 that there was an *ara Augusti Liburniae* probably at Scardona.

Together with the common fundamental organisation of the Concilia there were considerable varieties of detail corresponding to different conditions in East and West, and in considering No. 35 some of the more important of these may be noticed by way of contrast.

From the first section of the fragment, which deals with the duties and privileges of the priest and his wife, it is clear that in the West the priesthood was essentially Roman in character and modelled on the *flamonium Diale*. (Contrast with this the characteristic development of the Asiarchs, &c., in the Hellenistic part of the Empire. Mommsen, *Prov.* i. 345.) Like the *flamen Dialis,* the priest of Rome and Augustus is attended on public occasions by a lictor (l. 2), he has a seat and a vote in the local senate (l. 4), his official dress is the *praetexta* (l. 16. For the last two points in the case of the *flamen Dialis* cf. Liv. 27. 8. 7), and from the fragment relating to the priestess (6–8), who corresponds to the *flaminica Dialis*, it may be inferred that the traditional rules of conduct which bound the priest of Jupiter applied to him also (l. 7, cf. Gellius, 10. 15. 5: *iurare Dialem fas nunquam est ... mortuum nunquam attingit ... eaedem ferme cacrimoniae sunt, flaminicae Dialis*). For the special permission to the priestess to be present at spectacles cf. Suet. *Aug.* 44: *feminis ne gladiatores quidem . . . nisi ex superiore loco spectare concessit. Solum virginibus Vestalibus locum in theatro . . . dedit.*

The *ius signandi* of l. 15 probably refers to some method of voting by ballot (*per tabellam scilicet signatam.* Mommsen, *C. I. L.* xii. p. 864*), and with [*per tabell*]*as iurati* in l. 11 is illustrated by the method of voting in the κοινὸν Θεσσαλῶν, μεθ' ὅρκου κρύφα (Inscription of Kierion. Le Bas, iii. No. 1189. 2).

The section beginning with l. 17 refers not to absence from the city but to loss of citizenship. (Hirschfeld, *Zeitschrift der Savigny-Stiftung*, ix. (1888), *Röm. Abth.* 403. In the Digest *in civitate esse desinere* is used regularly in this technical sense which moreover includes the other case in which a new appointment would have to be made, that of death. Cf. *Dig.* 34. 1. 3: *ut quisque ex libertis decesserit aliove quo modo in civitate esse desierit.*)

The clause relating to the election of the priest has been lost, but cf. *C. I. L.* xii. 392: [*sacerdoti*] *templi divi* [*Aug(usti*) *quod est Nar*]*bone in quod* [*sacerdotium uni*]*versa provin*[*cia consentiente adl*]*ectus est.* The priests were universally taken from those who had attained the highest municipal rank. (Nos. 36, 37, 17, illustrate the regular formula: *omnibus honoribus apud suos functus.* Cf. p. 18.) It will be noticed (l. 22 sqq.) that the Concilium is to meet at Narbo only. In Asia the intense city-rivalries resulted in characteristic variations on both points. It is probable that the κοινόν there voted a list of names from which the final selection was made by the Proconsul; and the annual meeting came to be held, not as at first at Pergamum, but at the chief cities in rotation, each of which in consequence contained its own temple with a local ἀρχιερεύς who even assumed the title of 'Ασιάρχης.

The other inscriptions refer to the financial organisation

connected with the treasury of the Gauls (*arca Galliarum*. Cf. Mommsen, *Prov.* i. 95, note 1) or common fund contributed by the communities of the province for the maintenance of the worship and annual festival (No. 35, 36. 25) and other expenses authorised by the Concilium (e. g. *legationes*, Tac. *Ann.* 15. 22. 2). On the *cura* mentioned in No. 37 see Mommsen, *Prov.* i. 94 note.

The share taken by the Concilia in provincial administration, and the control which they came to exercise over the governor, are described by Mommsen, *Prov.* i. 94. The principal piece of evidence is the Inscription of Torigny (third cent., Mommsen, *Sitzungsberichte der Sächs. Gesell.* 1852, 235. Desjardins, *Gaule*, ii. 198. Hardy, *Provincial Concilia*, 250).

O. Hirschfeld, *Zur Geschichte des römischen Kaisercultus. Sitzungsberichte der k. pr. Akademie der Wissenschaften zu Berlin*, 1888, 833.

E. G. Hardy, *The Provincial Concilia from Augustus to Diocletian. English Historical Review*, 1890, 221.

P. Monceaux, *De Communi Asiae provinciae*, Paris, 1885.

The Worship of Augustus in Italy.

38.

C. I. L. x. 8375. Found at Cumae, in three fragments. Now in the Museum at Naples. Various small errors of the original are corrected in the text given below. Fully discussed by Mommsen, *Hermes*, xvii. (1882), 631.

9
[*XIIII K. Septembr. eo die Caesar pri*]mum consulatum in[*iit* . . . .]

3
[*III Non. Semptembr. eo die exer*]citus Lepidi tradidit se Caesari. Suppli[*c*]a[*tio* . .]

23.
[*VIIII K. Octobr. n*]atalis Caesaris. Immolatio Caesari hostia. Supplicatio . . .

7.
Nonis Octobr. Drusi Caesaris natalis. Supplicatio Vestae.

18. 5
XV K. Novembr. eo die Caesar togam virilem sumpsit. Supplicatio Spei et Iuve[*ntuti.*]

16.
XVI K. Decembr. natalis Ti. Caesaris. Supplicatio Vestae.

Dec. 15.   XVIII K. Ianuar. eo die a[*r*]a Fortunae Reducis dedicatast
            quae Caesarem [*ex transmari-*]
            nis provincis red[*uxit*].   Supplicatio Fortunae Reduci.

Jan. 7.   VII Idus Ianuar. e[*o die Caesar*] primum fasces sumpsit.
            Supplicatio Iovi sempi[*terno.*]

Jan. 5. 10 [*XV*]III K. Febr. eo di[*e Caesar Augustu*]s appellatus
            est.   Supplicatio Augusto.

Jan. 30.   [*III K. Febr. eo die ara Pacis Aug(ustae) dedicata*] est.
            Supplicatio imperio Caesaris Augusti cust[*odis*]
            [*civium Romanorum totiusque orbis terrar*]um.

Mar. 6.   [*Prid. Non. Mart. eo die Caesar pontifex ma*]ximus
            creatus est.   Supplicatio Vestae, dis pub(licis) P(ena-
            tibus) p(opuli) R(omani) Q(uiritium).

Apr. 14.   [*XVIII K. Mai. eo die Caesar primum vicit. Suppli*]catio
            Victoriae Augustae.

Apr. 15. 15 [*XVII K. Mai. eo die Caesar primum imperator app*]ellatus
            est.   Supplicatio Felicitati Imperi.

May 12.   [*IIII Id. Mai. eo die aedes Martis dedicatast. Supplica*]tio
            Molibus Martis.

May 24.   [*VIIII K. Iun. natalis Germanici Caesaris. Supp*]licatio
            Vestae.

July 12.   [*IIII Id. Iul. natalis divi Iuli. Supplicatio Iov*]i, Marti
            Ultori, Veneri [*Genetrici*].
            . . . . *Suppli*]catio Iovi . . . . .

l. 1. Aug. 19 is the New Year's Day. The beginning of the inscription has
been lost, but except the Consulship, there is no event in the life of Augustus,
falling between July 12 and Aug. 19, of sufficient importance to occupy the
position. The capture of Alexandria occurred on Aug. 1 (*C. I. L.* i. p. 398), but
it is unlikely that that was commemorated here when the victory of Actium was
passed over. Tacitus then is only adopting the view of Augustus himself as to
the starting-point of his official career, when he says of his death on Aug. 19,
Ann. 1. 9 : *idem dies accepti quondam imperii princeps et vitae supremus.*

l. 2. The day is supplied from the entry in the *Fasti Amiternini* for Sept. 3
(*C. I. L.* i. p. 324) : *Feriae) et supplicationes aput omnia pulvinaria quod eo die
Caes(ar) divi f. vicit in Sicilia.* The only victory of Augustus commemorated.
It is apparently selected because the defeat of Sextus Pompeius and the fall of
Lepidus restored peace to South Italy.

l. 3. The only *immolatio* in the Calendar, marking out Augustus as the central object of the worship.

l. 4. Drusus, son of Tiberius. The *Supplicatio Vestae* on the birthdays of members of the family of Augustus is explained by the Emperor's connection with her as Pontifex Maximus, and the presence of a temple to her within the Palatium. Ovid, *Met.* 15. 864: *Vestaque Caesareos inter sacrata penates. Fast.* 4. 949: *cognati Vesta recepta est limine.* Dio Cass. 54. 27. 3. *C. I. L.* i. p. 392 (Apr. 28).

l. 7. *Mon. Anc.* 2. 29: [*Aram Fortunae reduci iuxta ae*]*des Honoris et Virtutis ad portam* [*Capenam pro reditu meo se*]*natus consecravit,* B.C. 19. For other references see Mommsen, *Res Gest.* 46.

l. 9. *Lex Arae Narbonensis* (*C. I. L.* xii. 4333, Bruns, *Fontes,* p. 285) 25 : *VII quoq(ue` Idus Ianuar. qua die primum imperium orbis terrarum auspicatus est.* Cic. *Phil.* 11. 8. 20: *C. Caesari . . . fasces senatus dedit.* Tac. *Ann.* 1. 10: *ubi decreto patrum fasces et ius praetoris invaserit.* Cf. *Mon. Anc.* 1. 3.

l. 10. *Mon. Anc.* 6. 16: (on the *restitutio reipublicae* in B.C. 28–27) *quo pro merito meo senatu*[*s consulto Aug(ustus) appe*]*llatus sum.*

l. 11. B.C. 13. *Mon. Anc.* 2. 37: [*cu*]*m ex H*[*ispa*]*nia Gal*[*liaque, rebus in his p*]*rovincis prosp*[*e*]*re* [*gest*]*i̱ s,* R[*omam redi*] *Ti. Ne*[*r*]*one P. Qui*[*ntilio consulibu*]*s, aram* [*Pacis A*]*u*[*g*]*ust*[*ae senatus pro*] *redi*[*t*]*u meo co*[*nsecrari censuit*] *ad cam*[*pum Martium*]. For *custodis,* &c. cf. *C. I. L.* xi. 1421. 8 = *D.* 140, II. 9 (*Cenotaphia Pisana*) where Augustus is described as *custodis imperi Romani totiusque orbis terrarum praesidis.*

l. 13. B.C. 12. Cf. *Mon. Anc.* 2. 25. Dio Cass. 54. 27. 2. *C. I. L.* i. p. 387, and v. sup. l. 4.

l. 14. Ovid, *Fast.* 4. 627: (April 14) *hac Mutinensia Caesar grandine militia contudit arma sua.* Dio Cass. 46. 37. 3 : (Ἀντώνιος) τὸν Οὐίβιον πλησιάζοντα αἰσθόμενος, προσέβαλε πρὸς τὸ ἔρυμα τῶν ἀντικαθεστηκότων (Octavianus and Hirtius), εἴ πως προεξελὼν αὐτὸ ῥᾷον τοῦ λοιποῦ πολεμήσειεν.

l. 15. During the battle at Forum Gallorum (Cic. *ad Fam.* 10. 30) the camp of Octavianus was attacked by L. Antonius, as his brother had directed (Dio Cass. 46. 37. 4). For the results of the fighting on April 15 cf. Cic. *Phil.* 14. 10. 28 : (*C. Caesar) castra multarum legionum paucis cohortibus tutatus est, secundumque proelium fecit. Ita trium imperatorum virtute consilio felicitate uno die locis pluribus res publica est conservata.* Dio Cass. 46. 38 : αὐτοκράτορες οὐ μόνον ὁ Ἴρτιος ἀλλὰ καὶ ὁ Οὐίβιος καίπερ κακῶς ἀπαλλάξας, ὅ τε Καῖσαρ καίτοι μηδὲ μαχεσάμενος, καὶ ὑπὸ τῶν στρατιωτῶν καὶ ὑπὸ τῆς βουλῆς ὠνομάσθησαν.

l. 16. The reference to Mars suggests May 12, when there were *ludi* at Rome to commemorate the dedication of the temple of Mars Ultor on the Capitol in B.C. 20. *C. I. L.* i. p. 393. The only other reference to *Moles Martis* is in the catalogue of goddesses given by Gellius (13. 23) as invoked *in libris sacerdotum populi Romani et in plerisque antiquis orationibus . . . . Moles Martis.*

l. 17. The *supplicatio Vestae* shows that the commemoration is for the birthday of a member of the Imperial family. That of Germanicus is known from the *Acta Fratrum Arvalium* for A.D. 38. *C. I. L.* vi. 2028c 29, p. 468. Henzen, p. 52.

39.

C. I. L. x. 887, 888, 890.   Three of a number of inscriptions (*C. I. L.* x. p. 109 sqq.) from Pompeii, now in the Naples Museum, recording dedications made annually by the Ministri Mercurii Maiae (later Ministri Augusti), extending from B. C. 25 to A. D. 40.   The date of No. 41 is B. C. 2.   Nothing is known of the officials mentioned in No. 41. 9–11 as joining in the authorisation given by the chief magistrates of the town.   The interpretation of l. 11 is that suggested by Mommsen in *C. I. L.* x. p. 109.   It is very rare to find the *praenomen* following the *nomen*, as in Nos. 39 and 41.

IIO · SITTI · M · S ·

S · SORN · T · S

⌐A · VOLVSI · T · S ·

*minist*RI · MERC · MAI

5 *S*ACR · IVSSV

II · CELERIS

..... *Sitti M(arci) s(ervus),* ..... *Sorn(i) T(iti) s(ervus),* ...... *Volusi T(iti) s(ervus),* [*minist*]*ri Merc(uri) Mai(ae),* [*s*]*acr(um) iussu* ..... *Celeris* ...

40.

GRATVS · ARRI

MESSIVS · ARRIVS

INVENTVS

MEMOR · ISTACID

5 *mi*N · AVG · MERC · MAI

ex D · D · IVSSV

MARCEL

Gratus Arri (servus), Messius Arrius Inventus, Memor Istacid(i) (servus), [*mi*]*n(istri) Aug(usti) Merc(uri) Mai(ae),* [*ex*] *d(ecreto) d(ecurionum) iussu* ..... *Marcel(li)* ....

41.

A · VEIVS · PHYLAX

N · POPIDIVS · MOSCHVs

T · MESCINIVS · AMPHIO

```
        PRIMVS · ARRVNTI · M · S ·
  5     MIN · AVG · EX · D · D · IVSSV
        M · HOLCONI · RVFI · IV̄
        A · CLODI · FLACCI · IIĪ
              D · V · I · D ·
        P · CAESETI · POSTVMI
 10     N ·    TINTIRI ·    RVFI
        d V · V · A · S · P · P
        imp. caeSARE · XIIĪ ·
                                   CoS
        m. plautio siLVANO .
```

*A(ulus) Veius Phylax, N(umerius) Popidius Moschus, T(itus)
Mescinius Amphio, Primus Arrunti M(arci) s(ervus), min(istri)
Aug(usti) ex d(ecreto) d(ecurionum) iussu M(arci) Holconi
Rufi IV, A(uli) Clodi Flacci III, d(uum) v(irorum) i(ure)
d(icundo), P(ubli) Caeseti Postumi, N(umeri) Tintiri Rufi,
[d(uum)] v(irorum) v(otis) A(ugustalibus) s(acris) p(ublice)
p(rocurandis), [Imp(eratore) Cae]sare XIII [M(arco) Plautio
Si]lvano co(n)s(ulibus).*

42.

C. I. L. x. 820.   At Pompeii in the temple of Fortune.

M · TVLLIVS · M · F · D · V · I · D · TER · QVINQ · AVGVR · TR · MIL
Á · POP · AEDEM · FORTVNAE · AVGVST · SOLO · ET · PEQ · SVA

*M. Tullius M. f., d(uum) v(ir) i(ure) d(icundo) ter, quin-
q(uennalis), augur, tr(ibunus) mil(itum) a pop(ulo), aedem
Fortunae August(ae) solo et peq(unia) sua.*

43.

C. I. L. x. 837.   On the pedestal of a statue erected in the large theatre at
Pompeii.   Now in the Naples Museum.   The date is fixed by No. 41 to b.c. 2.

M · HOLCONIO · RVFO · D · V · I · D · IIII · QVINQ
TRIB · MIL · A · POPVLO · AVGVSTI · SACERDOTI
              EX · D · D ·

M. Holconio Rufo, d(uum) v(iro) i(ure) d(icundo) IIII, quin-

q(uennali), trib(uno) mil(itum) a populo, Augusti sacerdoti, ex
d(ecreto) d(ecurionum).

44.

C. I. L. x. 1613.   Formerly on the frieze of the Temple of Augustus at Puteoli.
The last words are d(e) s(uo) f(ecit).

l · cALPVRNIVS · L · F · TEMPLVM · AVGVSTO · CVM ·
ORNAMENTIS · D · S · F

The historians, from Tacitus onwards, are either silent
about a worship of Augustus in Italy, or else imply that
it was forbidden. Dio Cassius for instance, after describing
the inauguration of the provincial worship in Asia and Bithynia and its extension to the rest of the Empire (51. 20. 7,
quoted on p. 48), continues, ἐν γάρ τοι τῷ ἄστει αὐτῷ τῇ τε
ἄλλῃ Ἰταλίᾳ οὐκ ἔστιν ὅστις τῶν (αὐτοκρατόρων) καὶ ἐφ' ὁποσονοῦν
λόγου τινὸς ἀξίων ἐτόλμησε τοῦτο ποιῆσαι (cf. Tac. Ann. 1. 10. 5;
Suet. Aug. 52). The evidence, however, of contemporary
inscriptions shows that there existed in Italy a worship of
Augustus in his lifetime, of local origin and unequal distribution, but more direct and personal than the organised
devotion of the provinces. The statement of Dio is perfectly
true if taken of the contrast between Augustus and all the
other Emperors, and not as applying to him among the rest,
for, with the exception of a few instances of a worship of
Tiberius (C. I. L. ix. 652, x. 688, iv. 1180?), Augustus stands
alone among the Emperors as the recipient of divine honours
in his lifetime in Italy. The worship is local, for while all
Italy welcomed the rule of Augustus, there were places and
persons whose loyalty had not risen to the point of giving
him divine honours, and in some cases there might be positive opposition to such an innovation (cf. Tac. Ann. 1. 10. 5).
On the other hand where an individual or a community was
in some special relation to Augustus, or was less subject to
conservative Roman prejudices, a favourable soil was provided.

Apparently this was peculiarly the case in Campania, with its settlements of the veterans of Augustus (p. 34), and the Greek element in its towns. For the latter point Pompeii is typical. Yet even here we see the cult beginning in indirect and tentative forms, and only gradually becoming more direct and outspoken. (1) In B.C. 25 we find in existence *a collegium* of worshippers of Mercurius and Maia (No. 39). Later (No. 40 is undated) Augustus is associated with them (the connection is illustrated by Hor. 1 *C.* 2. 41), and in B.C. 2 he has displaced the other divinities and appears alone (No. 41). (2) A temple of Fortuna Augusta was erected by a private individual on the site of a private house (see the plan of Pompeii e. g. in Overbeck, and compare with the position of the official temples in the Forum). The dedicatory inscription (No. 42) was withdrawn from public view by being inscribed, not in the regular place, on the epistyle facing the street, but within the cella above the niche where the image stood (for other indications see Nissen l. c. infr.). The date of the foundation is unknown, but in A.D. 3 a *collegium* of *ministri* was instituted in connection with the temple (*C. I. L.* x. 824). (3) Any reserve which may be inferred from the evidence just given had become unnecessary by B.C. 2 when, as No. 43 shows, a public devotion to Augustus was in existence, and its priesthood recognised as practically part of the local *cursus honorum*, and filled by one of the leading men of the place.

We have no evidence of any such process of development in the case of the temple of Augustus erected by a private founder at Puteoli (No. 44). The high water mark of Campanian devotion was reached at Cumae, where, as we learn from the document known as the 'Feriale Cumanum' (No. 38), there was a temple of Augustus, the worship of which was organised on the basis of a special sacred year, all the holy days of which commemorated events in the life of Augustus, or the birthdays of members of his family.

The following is a list of the places in Italy in addition
to those mentioned above, where there is evidence for a
worship of Augustus. In nearly every case, as O. Hirschfeld
has shown (*Kaisercultus, Sitzungsber. der Berlin. Akad.* 1888,
838), some connection can be proved between Augustus and
the community. Asisium (*C. I. L.* xi. 5175 : *flamen Aug. paren-
tis municipi*), Beneventum (*C. I. L.* ix. 1556 : *Caesareum Imp.
Caesari Augusto et coloniae Beneventanae*), Fanum Fortunae
(Vitruvius, 5. 1. 7 : *aedes Augusti*), Pisa (*C. I. L.* xi. 1420=*D.*
139 : *Augusteum*, 1421. 43=*D.* 140. ii. 43 : *flamen Augustalis*),
Tibur (or perhaps Tuder, *C. I. L.* xiv. 3590: *flamen August(alis)*),
Verona (*C. I. L.* v. 3341 : *flam(ini) Aug(usti) primo Veron(ae)
creato.* Cf. 3376, 3936), an unidentified town of Latium (*C. I. L.*
xiv. 3500: *flamen Augusta[lis]*), and possibly Ancona (*C. I. L.*
ix. 5904: [*sacerdoti Au*]*g(usti) Victoriae Caesaris.* Cf. *C. I. L.*
i, p. 397: *ludi Victoriae Caesaris*). The *ara numinis Augusti*
at Forum Clodii, the worship of which is regulated by decrees
of A. D. 18 (*C. I. L.* xi. 3303 = *D.* 154), seems to have been
in existence for some time, and probably dates from the lifetime of Augustus (l. c. 4 : *victimae natali Aug. VIII K.
Octobr. duae quae p(er)p(etuo) inmolari adsuetae sunt*).

Mommsen, *das Augustische Festverzeichniss von Cumae. Hermes,* xvii. (1882),
631.

Nissen, *Pompeianische Studien,* 183.

The Vicomagistri and the Worship of the Lares Augusti at Rome.

45.

C. I. L. vi. 448. On an altar from Rome, now at Florence. Parts of the
inscription are preserved by copies made when it was in a more perfect state.
(*a*) is on the front of the altar with three figures (two male, one female)
apparently engaged in sacrifice. (*b*) is on the right face of the altar with a
representation of the two Lares of the ordinary type. The date is B.C. 2. In
l. 2 Ɔ = *Gaia* which is always used in describing a freedman who has been
manumitted by a woman. The line reads thus : *D(ecimus) Oppius (mulieris)*

l(ibertus) Iaso, De(cimus) Lucilius D(ecimi) l(ibertus) Salvius, L. Brinnius (muli-eris) l(ibertus) Princeps, L. Furius L. l(ibertus) Salvius, mag(istri) vici Sandaliari.

(*a*) IMP · CAESARE AVGVSTO X̅I̅I̅I̅ M · PLAVTIO
    SILVAN COS ·
    D OPPIVS · Ɔ · L · IASÓ · D · LVCILIVS · D ·
    L · SALVIVS · L · BRINNIVS · Ɔ · L · PRINCEPS ·
    L · FV́RIVS · L · L · SALVIVS
         MAG · VICI · SANDALIARI

(*b*)   LARIBVS · AVGVSTIS

Augustus did not consider it advisable to initiate or permit a direct worship of himself in the capital (Suet. *Aug.* 52 : *in urbe pertinacissime abstinuit hoc honore*). But as it was important that the lower classes there, no less than the wealthy freedmen and the upper ranks of the provincials, should be made familiar with the ideas of which the Imperial cult was the symbol, when Augustus in B.C. 12-7 (*C. I. L.* vi. p. 86) restored and remodelled the old organisation of the *vicus* for purposes of local government in Rome (the *vicomagistri*), he at the same time reconstituted the old worship round which that organisation had centred, in such a way that it should serve the same purpose as the forms of the Imperial cult outside Rome. Henceforward the *Lares compitales*, the protecting deities of the *vicus*, honoured at its centre the *compitum* (Jordan, *Topographie der Stadt Rom.* i. 534, ii. 50–53. Hence Plin. *H. N.* 3. 66: *regiones XIV compita larium CCLXV*, meaning the 265 *vici* of Augustus), are replaced by the *Lares Augusti*, and with them the *Genius Augusti* is associated.

The following is the most probable account of the history and meaning of this transformation. Originally we find a pair of Lares protecting the *vicus*, and a single Lar protecting the house (*Lar familiaris* or *domesticus*). By the time of Cicero the Lar of the house was replaced by a pair of Lares (e.g. Cic. *de Domo*, 41. 108, &c.) represented like those of the *vicus* or *compitum*. For the identity of representation cf. Naevius, ap. Fest. p. 230 = Merry, *Fragments*, p. 24: *Theodotum compiles qui aris Compitalibus* ... *Lares ludentis pinxit*, and the common representations in houses at Pompeii of the Lares with elevated drinking-horn and *patera* or *situla*, which are precisely similar to those of the *Lares compitales* in the streets. Helbig, *Wandgemälde*, p. 13, and compare *fig.* 1888 article *Compitum* in Daremberg and Saglio, *Dict. Ant.*, with the ordinary type of *Lares domestici*, e.g. Baumeister, *Denkmäler*, p. 811. With these other deities were commonly associated but still more regularly the Genius (Helbig gives fifteen cases of the Lares and Genius at Pompeii as against six cases of the Lares alone. *Wandg.* pp. 12 and 14, and cf. list with additional instance in the *Annali*, 1872, p. 32), and there was a tendency to identify the latter with the paterfamilias for the time being, i. e. the representation of the Genius took the form of a portrait. (Instances in Helbig, e. g. p. 11. 31: 'der trefflich erhaltene Kopf des Genius zeigt den römischen Portraittypus des ersten Kaiserzeit.') If we suppose that the house of Augustus had its *Lares (domus) Augusti*, with whom the *Genius Augusti* would be associated, it would not be unnatural that the restoration of the *Lares compitales* with the objects stated above should take the form of identifying them with the *Lares domestici* of the author of the restored worship and of the organisation connected with it; while the practice of joining the Genius with the Lares will account for the association of the *Genius Augusti.* (Ovid, *Fast.* 5. 145: *mille Lares Geniumque ducis qui tradidit illos Urbs habet et vici numina trina colunt.*) Such a step was made easier by (1) the identity of representation between the *Lares compitales* and the *Lares domestici*, and (2) the practice of worshipping Augustus or his Genius under the form of a portrait, in private oratories (Hor. 4 *C.* 5. 34: *Laribus tuum miscet numen*).

It is not, however, clear that the *Genius Augusti* was at first officially united with the *Lares Augusti* or *Compitales* as they are henceforward indifferently called (cf. Suet. *Aug.* 31). Ovid (l. c.) is the only writer who refers to the *numina trina*, whereas Suetonius, &c., mention simply the Lares, and the regular type of dedication under the early Empire is *Laribus Augustis* (e. g. No. 45. The only exception is *C. I. L.* vi. 445 [B.C. 7], *G*[*enio Caesaru*]*m*, which Jordan (*Vesta und die Laren,* 15) restored thus: *Laribus Augusti G*[*enio Caesaris*]. The presence of the *Genius Augusti* is perhaps implied in one or two other cases, e. g. *C. I. L.* vi. 448, *Bull. Comunale,* 1888, 327) as contrasted with *Laribus Augustis et Geniis Caesarum* (*Genio Imperatoris*) from the end of the first century onwards (*C. I. L.* vi. 449–452. *Eph. Epigr.* iv. 746, 747).

For the institution of the *magistri* cf. Suet. *Aug.* 30 : *spatium urbis in regiones vicosque divisit instituitque ut . . . hos magistri e plebe cuiusque viciniae lecti (tuerentur).* Dio Cass. 55. 8. 7 (B.C. 7): καί σφισι καὶ τῇ ἐσθῆτι τῇ ἀρχικῇ καὶ ῥαβδού-χοις δύο ἐν αὐτοῖς τοῖς χωρίοις ὧν ἂν ἄρχωσιν, ἡμέραις τισὶ χρῆσθαι ἐδόθη, ἥ τε δουλεία ἡ τοῖς ἀγορανόμοις τῶν ἐμπιπραμένων ἕνεκα συνοῦσα ἐπετράπη. As we see from No. 45 they were generally freedmen. They are mentioned by Dio apparently in connection with the precautions against fire, and perhaps the administration of the *vici* of Rome was at first entrusted to them (the references to the *vici* are few, e. g. Suet. *Aug.* 40 : *populi recensum vicatim egit.* 43 : *fecit nonnunquam vicatim* [*ludos*]), but after the establishment of the *praefectura vigilum* in A. D. 6 (Dio Cass. 55. 26. 4) and the centralisation of authority at Rome in the later years of Augustus in the hands of the *praefectus urbis* with the *cohortes urbanae* at his disposal (cf. Tac. *Ann.* 6. 10. 5, *Hist.* 3. 64), they practically disappear except for religious purposes. They are mentioned Suet. *Tib.* 76 : *dedit et legata plerisque . . . atque etiam separatim vicorum magistris ;* but cf. *Claud.* 18 : (during a great fire) *deficiente militum ac familiarum turba, auxilio plebem per magistratus ex omnibus vicis convocavit.*

The identification of the *Lares Augusti* with the *Lares domestici* of Augustus was originally suggested by Reifferscheid, *Annali dell' Instituto*, 1863, 121, esp. 133. It was accepted with modifications by Jordan, *Vesta und die Laren*, 15 ; *Annali*, 1872, 28 sqq.

The Augustales.

46.

C. I. L. ii. 1944. From Suel in Baetica. l. 6 : *d(ecurionum) d(ecreto)*. l. 9 : *d(e) s(ua) p(ecunia) d(edit) d(edicavit)*.

```
        NEPTVNO  ·  AVG
            SACRVM
     L · IVNIVS · PVTEOLANVS
       V̄I · VIR · AVGVSTALIS
   5  IN   MVNICIPIO  ·  SVELITANO
      D · D · PRIMVS · ET · PERPETVVS
      OMNIBVS · HONORIBVS · QVOS
      LIBERTINI · GERERE · POTVERVN̄
      HONORATVS·EPVLO·DATO·D·S·P·D·D
```

47.

C. I. L. x. 4792. At Tiano (Teanum Sidicinum). l. 3 : *H. S. sexaginta millia.*

```
     S · C · BALNEVM · CLODIANVM
     EMPTVM · CVM · SVIS · AEDIFICIS
     EX · PECVNIA · AVGVSTAL · HS · 𐆖𐆖
     Q  ·   MINVCI    IKARI
  5  C  ·   AVFILLI   SVAVIS
     C  ·   AISCIDI   LEPOTIS
     N     HERENNI    OPTATI
     M  ·  CAEDI      CHILONIS
     M  ·  OVINI      FAVSTI
```

48.

C. I. L. v. 6349. Found at Lodi Vecchio (Laus Pompeia) and preserved there.

HERC · SAC

M MASCARPIVS

SYMPHORIO

VIVIR   ·   SEN

5   ET · AVG · C · D · D

ORNAM   ·   DEC

AB ORD SPLENDID

M̄ M̄ HONOR

CVM MASCARPIO

10   FESTO · FILIO

EQ · R EQ · P

VI · VIR · IVN · DEC

VOT · SOL

*Herc(uli) sac(rum). M. Mascarpius Symphorio VIvir sen(ior)
et Aug(ustalis) c(reatus) d(ecurionum) d(ecreto), ornam(entis)
dec(urionalibus) ab ord(ine) splendid(issimo) m(unicipum)
M(ediolaniensium) honor(atus), cum Mascarpio Festo filio,
eq(uite) R(omano) eq(uo) p(ublico), VIvir(o) iun(iore), de-
c(urione), vot(um) sol(vit).*

In the Provincial Concilia and the Magistri Vicorum at
Rome we have had two illustrations of the policy of Augustus
in providing classes excluded from the higher ranks of public
life with spheres of administrative activity by means of or-
ganisations which at the same time bound them to the worship
of the Emperor and the Imperial system.   It is the same
idea which underlies the institution of the Augustales.   As
the Concilia affected the upper class of provincials, and the
worship of the Lares Augusti, the lower orders of the capital,
so the *Augustalium ordo* gave a kind of official status to the
principal class which was excluded from municipal honours
in the towns of Italy and the (Latin) provinces, the freedmen.

There is no direct evidence that Augustus founded the institution, but there can be little doubt that it is due to him, for the earliest instances belong to his time (cf. *C. I. L.* xi. 3805 inf., Allmer, *Lyon*, ii. p. 376), and its general diffusion in the West (with the exception of Africa) points to some action by the Imperial government. With certain local varieties of detail the same general features are found everywhere. Six persons (*sexviri, seviri*) nearly always freedmen, are annually nominated by the municipal Senate to superintend the worship of the Emperor. After their year of office they pass into the *ordo*, the general name for the members of which was *Augustales*. The fact that the primary intention of the whole institution was the worship of the Emperor, is illustrated by *C. I. L.* x. 1877 (from Puteoli of A.D. 176): *D(is) M(anibus). Q. Insteio Diadumeno, Augustali, coluit annis XXXXV, &c.* The normal usage as to title is that given above, but there is considerable local variation. Thus in South Italy, *Augustalis*, the general descriptive title of the whole organisation, is used of the *seviri* as well as of the members of the *ordo* (No. 47, where it will be observed that each *sevir* contributes HS 10,000 to the total), whereas in Gaul the converse is the case, i. e. the particular title of the annual officials is retained after office just as in the fuller form *sevir (et) Augustalis*. It is probable that at first admission into the *ordo* after the year of office was a special privilege conferred by the *decuriones*, which later became universal, or rather the *ordo* originated in the practice of allowing some *seviri* to retain the insignia of their position for life. Hence we get such forms as *sevir perpetuus* (in Spain, exactly corresponding to *Augustalis perpetuus*, e. g. at Olisipo *C. I. L.* ii. 83 = *D.* 5640), *vi vir Augustalis creatus decreto decurionum* (at Mediolanum, No. 48, *C. I. L.* v. 5844), and more commonly *sevir et Augustalis* (esp. in Central and North Italy), which becomes finally *sevir Augustalis*. Such an expression as *sex vir et sex vir Augustalis* (*C. I. L.* xi. 6306 = *D.* 5445) is consequently redundant, for the *seviratus* is implied in the last part. The *ordo*, which is analogous to the *equester ordo* at Rome, only implies a recognised social rank, and must be distinguished from anything of the nature of a *corpus* or *collegium*, which occurs only rarely in the case of the Augustales (*Augustales corporati*).

Augustales were sometimes admitted directly into the *ordo* without having passed through the *seviratus*. A decree of the Senate of Veii of A.D. 26 (*C.I.L.* xi. 3805 = *D.* 6579) illustrates the sort of grounds on which this was done : *placuit . . . ex auctoritate omnium permitti C. Iulio divi Augusti l(iberto) Geloti qui omni tempore municip(ium) Veios non solum consilio et gratia adiuverit sed etiam impensis suis et per filium suum celebrari voluerit honorem ei iustissimum decerni ut Augustalium numero habeatur aeque ac si eo honore usus sit.* The *Augustalitas* was not a stepping-stone to the municipal magistracies, and the highest dignity that an Augustalis could hope for was the *ornamenta* (*aedilicia, duumviralia, decurionalia*) conferred by the *curia* as a special favour. At Mediolanum, however, *ingenui* as well as *liberti* obtained the *seviratus*, and the former after their year of office, during which they were called *seviri iuniores*, passed on to the municipal *honores* and a seat in the *curia*. The freedmen on the other hand, who are spoken of as *seviri seniores*, enter the *Augustalium ordo* in due course, and attain to nothing higher than the *ornamenta*. This is illustrated by No. 48, where we have a father belonging to one rank, and the son, in whose generation the taint of servile origin is lost, belonging to the other. (Mommsen in *C.I.L.* v. p. 635 and note, where evidence is given for the existence of a similar arrangement at a few other towns in North Italy.)

The *Augustalitas* not only satisfied the ambition of the freedmen by giving them a limited public career, but at the same time retained in the towns a class which was essential to their material prosperity, and exacted from it as the price of the dignity substantial contributions to the municipal funds (the *summa honoraria* on admission to the *seviratus*), as well as the undertaking of public works of ornament or utility (e.g. *C. I. L.* ix. 808 at Luceria two Augustales *pro munere* [*viam*] *sua pecunia straverunt*), not to speak of largesses and benefactions which were no doubt equally compulsory (e. g. *C. I. L.* ii. 2100 at Ossigi in Baetica: *sacrum Polluci Sex. Quintius Sex. Q(uintii) Successini lib(ertus) Fortunatus, ob honorem VI vir(atus), ex d(ecreto) ordinis soluta pecunia petente populo dorum de sua pecunia dato epulo civibus et incolis, et circensibus factis, d(edit) d(edicavit)*.) Petronius has left us in his Trimalchio a type of the class of wealthy freedmen who were willing to spend their money freely in the Italian and provincial towns in exchange for the rank and outward distinctions of the *Seviratus* and *Augustalitas* (cf. esp. Petr. *Cena Tr.* 71).

It seems probable that the origin of the Augustales is to be found in the *collegia* connected with the worship of Mercurius, with whom Augustus was associated (cf. p. 57). The two following inscriptions (not later than Augustus) illustrate the earliest stage : *C. I. L.* iii. 1769 (at Narona): *Aug(usto) sacr(um) C. Iulius Macrini lib. Martialis, IIIIII vir m(agister) M(ercurialis?), &c.* x. 1272 (at Nola): *L. Sattio L. l. magistro Mercuriali et Augustalei.*

For other inscriptions of Augustales, see Nos. 53, 95.

J. Schmidt, *De Seviris Augustalibus, Dissert. Halenses*, v. pt. 1, 1878. O. Hirschfeld, *Zeitschr. f. Oesterr. Gymn.* 1878, 289, differs from the views of Schmidt. Friedlaender, *Petronius Cena Trimalch. Introd.* 36–40.

PART II.

FROM THE DEATH OF AUGUSTUS TO THE ACCESSION OF VESPASIAN,
A. D. 14–69.

I. HISTORY OF THE EMPERORS AND PERSONS CONNECTED WITH THEM.

Position of Iulia Augusta.

49.

C. I. L. ii. 2038. From Antequera (Anticaria in Baetica). The reading of l. 4 is confirmed by No. 50. Erected between A.D. 14 and 29.

```
    IVLIAE  ·  AVG  ·  DRVSI ƒ. DIVi aug.
    MATRI · TI · CAESARIS · AVG · PRINCIPIS
    ET · CONSERVATORIS · ET · DRVSI · GER
    M A N I C I   ·   GENetrici   ·   O R B I S
5        M · CORNELIVS · PROCVLVS
         PONTVFEX · CAESARVM
```

50.

Cohen, i. p. 169, No. 3. Eckhel, vi. 154. Bronze medallion of the Colonia Iulia Romula (Hispalis). Cf. *B. M. C. Emp.* i, p. cxxxvi.

Obverse. PERM(*issu*) DIVI AVG. COL(*onia*) ROM(*ula*). Head of Augustus surrounded by rays.

Reverse. IVLIA AVGVSTA GENETRIX ORBIS. Head of Iulia.

51.

Cohen, i. p. 165, No. 807. Large bronze of Leptis in Africa. Cf. p. 207, No. 203, similar coin with *Imp. Tib. Caesar Aug. cos. V* on obverse. Eckhel, vi. 155.

Obv.   IMP. CAESAR AV(*gustus*).   Head of Augustus.
Rev.   AVGVSTA MATER PATRIAE.   Seated figure of Iulia.

Nos. 49–51 illustrate the statement of Dio Cassius (57. 12. 4): πολλοὶ μὲν μητέρα αὐτὴν τῆς πατρίδος, πολλοὶ δὲ καὶ γονέα προσαγορεύεσθαι γνώμην ἔδωκαν, and show that in spite of the refusal of Tiberius to ratify such honours decreed to his mother by the Senate (Dio Cass. l. c.), the provincial towns were at least not prohibited from conferring similar marks of distinction upon her.

Mommsen remarks (*St. R.* ii. 788, note 4) that with a weaker ruler than Tiberius, Iulia Augusta would have taken her place as practically the colleague of the Princeps. For references to her attempts to assert her claims to a share in the Government, cf. Dio Cass. 56. 47 : τῶν πραγμάτων ὡς καὶ αὐταρχοῦσα ἀντεποιεῖτο.   57. 12. 3 : πλήν τε ὅτι οὔτε ἐς τὸ συνέδριον οὔτε ἐς τὰ στρατόπεδα οὔτε ἐς τὰς ἐκκλησίας ἐτόλμησέ ποτε ἐσελθεῖν, τά γε ἄλλα πάντα ὡς καὶ αὐταρχοῦσα διοικεῖν ἐπεχείρει. Suet. *Tib.* 50 : *partes sibi aequas potentiae vindicans ;* and for the way in which they were repressed by Tiberius, Dio Cass. 57. 12. 5.   It is possible that Augustus may have intended her to occupy some such position, for the *nomen Augustum* which she was empowered to assume under his will (Tac. *Ann.* 1. 8. 2), properly belongs to the reigning Princeps (*St. R.* ii. 821).

Seianus.

52.

Cohen, i. p. 198, No. 97.   Eckhel, vi. 196.   Middle bronze of Bilbilis in Hispania Tarraconensis.

Obverse. TI. CAESAR DIVI AVGVSTI F. AVGVSTVS. Head of Tiberius.

Reverse. MVN(*icipium*) AVGVSTA BILBILIS TI. CAESARE V. L. AELIO SEIANO COS. The last word within an oak wreath.

53·

C.I.L. xi. 4170. Interamna (Terni) on the Nar. The date (A. D. 32) expressed by *ad* with the accusative is irregular. The name of the colleague of Cn. Domitius Ahenobarbus was Camillus Arruntius (better known as M. Furius Camillus Scribonianus) erased after his rebellion against Claudius in A. D. 42. The last words are *p(ecunia) s(ua) f(aciendum) c(uravit)*.

SALVTI · PERPETVAE · AVGVSTAE   GENIO · MVNICIPI · ANNO · POST
LIBERTATIQVE · PVBLICAE   INTERAMNAM · CONDITAM
POPVLI · ROMANI   ⅠƆCCIIII · AD · CN · DOMITIVM
   AHENOBARBVM *m. furium* COS
   camillum scribonianum

ᴘROVIDENTIAE · TI · CAESARIS · AVGVSTI · NATI · AD · AETERNITATEM
ROMANI · NOMINIS · SVBLATO · HOSTE · PERNICIOSISSIMO · P · R
FAVSTVS · TITIVS · LIBERALIS · VI · VIR · AVG · ITER
P · S · F · C

The coin No. 52 is quite as much a monument of the exceptional position to which Tiberius raised Sejanus, as of the adulation which that position brought him from provincial towns like Bilbilis. Tiberius was Consul only three times after becoming Emperor, twice in order to give to Germanicus and Drusus the prestige of having the Princeps as their colleague (A.D. 18 and 21), the third time in order to pay the same compliment to Sejanus (A.D. 31). Whether or not Tiberius intended to put him off his guard and keep him at Rome, as Suetonius suggests (*Tib.* 65), this was the highest mark of favour that he could confer short of making him his colleague in the Empire; and in the eyes of the world the inference would be that Sejanus had succeeded to the place formerly occupied by the sons and heirs-apparent of the Emperor. The people of Bilbilis commemorated the importance of the occasion by inscribing the name of Sejanus as well as that of his Imperial colleague on their coins of the year (No. 52). How exceptional the honour was, may be measured by the fact that in A.D. 18 they had omitted the name of the Emperor's colleague, Germanicus, though he was his adopted son (Cohen, i. p. 198, No. 96 : *Mun. Augusta Bilbilis Ti. Caesare III cos*). After the death of Sejanus on Oct. 18 (Tac. *Ann*. 6. 25. 4) his name was as far as possible erased from the coins. For instances of such erasure, see Eckhel, l. c.

There can be no doubt that the *hostis perniciosissimus* of No. 53 is Sejanus. It was erected the year after his fall and, as we might expect, by one specially interested in the welfare of the Imperial house, a *sevir Augustalis*.

Gaius and his Family.

54.

C. I. L. vi. 886, 887. The marble receptacles on which Nos. 54, 55 are inscribed, and which contained the actual ashes, were brought from the Mausoleum of Augustus to the Capitol in the fourteenth century. That of Agrippina may still be seen there in the courtyard of the Palace of the Conservatori. That of her son has disappeared.

OSSA

AGRIPPINAE · M · AGRIPPAE · *f*

DIVI · AVG · NEPTIS · VXORIS

GERMANICI · CAESARIS

5   MATRIS · C · CAESARIS · AVG

GERMANICI · PRINCIPIS

55.

OSSA

NERONIS · CAESARIS

GERMANICI · CAESARIS · F

DIVI · AVG · PRON · FLAMIN

5   AVGVSTALIS · QVAESTORIS

56.

C. I. L. vi. 882.   On the obelisk which stands in front of St. Peter's at Rome. Originally brought by Gaius from Egypt and placed in the Circus of his gardens on the Vatican (Plin. *H. N.* 16. 201), on the site of which it remained till moved to its present position in 1586.

DIVO · CAESARI · DIVI · IVLII · F · AVGVSTO
TI · CAESARI · DIVI · AVGVSTI · F · AVGVSTO
SACRVM

57.

B. M. C. Emp. i, Cal. 81.   Eckhel, vi. 213.   Large bronze issued under Gaius. The argument of Eckhel in favour of attributing all the memorial coins of Agrippina to Claudius on account of the mention of Agrippa (v. infr.), is refuted by No. 54.

Obverse. AGRIPPINA M. F. MAT. C. CAESARIS AVGVSTI. Head of Agrippina.

Reverse. S. P. Q. R. MEMORIAE AGRIPPINAE. Representation of a *carpentum* drawn by two mules.

One of the first acts of Gaius was to bring the remains of his mother from Pandateria the scene of her exile and death in A.D. 33 (Tac.*Ann.* 6. 25. Suet. *Tib.* 53), and those of his brother Nero from Pontia, where he had come to his end in A. D. 31 (Suet. *Tib.* 54). Suet. *Cal.* 15 : *confestim Pandateriam et Pontias ad transferendos matris fratrisque cineres festinavit, tempestate turbida, quo magis pietas emineret, adiitque vener-abundus ac per semet in urnas condidit; nec minore scaena Ostiam, praefixo in biremis puppe vexillo, et inde Romam Tiberi subvectos, per splendidissimum quemque equestris ordinis medio ac frequenti die duobus ferculis Mausoleo intulit.* The coin No. 57 is explained by the next words : *inferiasque is annua religione publice instituit et eo amplius matri Circenses carpen-tumque quo in pompa traduceretur.* The epitaph of Agrippina (No. 54) shows that the attitude towards his ancestor Agrippa attributed to Gaius by Suetonius was, quite characteristically, only a caprice (*Cal.* 23. Cf. his rehabilitation of Antonius at the expense of Augustus. Dio Cass. 59. 20; Suet. *Cal.* 23). The omission of Tiberius among the ancestors in his brother's epitaph (No. 55) is intentional and marked. Gaius after conducting his predecessor's funeral (Dio Cass. 59. 3; Suet. *Cal.* 15) had omitted his name from the annual *iusiurandum in acta* (Dio Cass. 59. 9, cf. p. 86), and lost no opportunity of vilifying him in public (id. 59. 16). But Dio (l. c.) shows that he was obliged to withdraw from this attitude which he no doubt began to feel was undermining the prestige of the Principate, and it is possible that the inscription on the Vatican obelisk (No. 56) may have been intended to let the world know his altered views. Certainly the honour is peculiar, and amounts practically to deification. (Mommsen on *C. I. L.* vi. 882 : *qualis consecrationis factae homini defuncto non relato inter divos alterum exemplum non facile reperias.*)

The Accession of Claudius : A.D. 41.

58.

B. M. C. Emp. i, Claud. 5.   Eckhel, vi. 235.   Aureus of A. D. 41.

Obverse. TI. CLAVD. CAESAR AVG. P. M. TR. P.   Head of Claudius.

Reverse. IMPER. RECEPT.   Representation of the Castra Praetoria at Rome.

59.

B. M. C. Emp. i, Claud. 8.   Eckhel, vi. 235.   Aureus of A. D. 41.

Obverse. TI. CLAVD. CAESAR AVG. P. M. TR. P.   Head of Claudius.

Reverse. PRAETOR. RECEPT.   Claudius giving his hand to a praetorian soldier who holds a standard.

These coins, coming from the Imperial mint, represent the

accession of Claudius from two points of view, (1) that of the Guards, and (2) that of the Emperor. The political results of the 'esprit de corps' generated among the Praetorians by their concentration in the permanent camp represented on No. 58 (cf. Tac. *Ann.* 4. 2), are illustrated by the legend *Imperatore recepto*, implying as it does that an Emperor was necessary for their continued existence. It is possible that the words may contain a further reference to the fact that Claudius, on his discovery, was carried off to the camp by the Guards and spent the first night of his reign there (Suet. *Cl.* 10: *receptus intra vallum, inter excubias militum pernoctavit*). On the other hand Claudius owed his elevation solely to the Guards, for the other part of the garrison of the capital, the *cohortes urbanae*, placed themselves in the first instance at the disposition of the Senate (Suet. l. c.: *consules cum senatu et cohortibus urbanis forum Capitoliumque occupaverant asserturi communem libertatem*). The scene of the taking of the *sacramentum* by the Praetorians (with *receptis* in No. 59 supply *in fidem*) was therefore a fitting memorial of the accession of the first Emperor who owed his position to them, and who recognised his obligation by a substantial reward. Suet. *Cl.* 10 : *armatos pro contione iurare in nomen suum passus est promisitque singulis quina dena sestertia, primus Caesarum fidem militis etiam praemio pigneratus.*

The Rise of Burrus: Sole Praefectus Praetorio : A.D. 51.

60.

C. I. L. xii. 5842. Found at Vaison (Vasio). The larger part is now in the Museum at Avignon.

VASIENS ❖ VOC
PATRÓNO
SEX ❖ AFRANIO ❖ SEX ❖ F ❖
VOLT ❖ BURRO

5   TRIB ⟡ MIL ⟡ PROC ⟡ AVGVS

TAE ⟡ PROC ⟡ TI · CAESAR

PROC ⟡ DIVI ⟡ CLAVDI

PRÁEF · PRA*e*TORI ⟡ ORNA

M*ent*Is ⟡ C O N S V L A R

· · · · · · · · ·

*Vasiens(es) Voc(ontii) patrono Sex. Afranio Sex. f.
Volt(inia) (tribu) Burro, trib(uno) mil(itum), proc(uratori)
Augustae, proc(uratori) Ti. Caesar(is), proc(uratori) divi Claudi,
praef(ecto) pra[é]tori, ornam[ent]is consular[ibus ornato. . . . . .]*

This inscription gives us the only information we possess
about the career of Burrus before he obtained the command
of the Guards in A.D. 51. As Vasio belonged to the Vol-
tinian tribe, it is probable that he was a native of the *civitas*
of which in the days of his greatness he became patron.
(For the Vasienses Vocontii, see p. 14.)   The steps in his
promotion illustrate the equestrian career in its earlier form,
starting with military service as a legionary tribune (*tribunus
militum angusticlavius*), passing into the personal service of
the Emperor as *procurator* of some part of his possessions,
and finally reaching the highest post open to an *eques*, that
of *praefectus praetorio*.   But the way in which the service of
the Emperors, including that of Augusta (i. e. Livia, the
mother of Tiberius) is here spoken of absolutely, with no
department specified, shows that the *procurator* is as yet
hardly an official, but only a private servant (cf. *C. I. L.* x.
7489 : *proc. Ti. Caesaris et Iuliae Augustae*).

The command of the Guards as instituted by Augustus
(Dio Cass. 52. 24) was, no doubt as a matter of precaution,
divided between two *praefecti* (in later times occasionally
three), and this arrangement was generally followed by his
successors, though apparently at the death of Augustus Seius
Strabo was in sole command (Tac. *Ann.* 1. 7. 3).   The reasons
which induced Agrippina to replace Lusius Geta and Rufrius

Crispinus by Burrus in A.D. 51 are stated by Tacitus,
Ann. 12. 42. He retained the position till his death in
A.D. 62, when the dual command was restored (Tac. *Ann.*
14. 51).

L. Verginius Rufus. Defeat of Vindex: A.D. 68.

61.

C. I. L. v. 5702. From the district S. of the lake of Como. Now in the
Brera at Milan.

IOVI · O · M
PRO   SALVTE
ET · VICTORIA · L
VERGINI   ·   RVFI
5   PYLADES · SALTVAR
V · S

*Iovi o(ptimo) m(aximo), pro salute et victoria L. Vergini
Rufi, Pylades saltuar(ius) v(otum) s(olvit).*

When C. Julius Vindex, the legatus of Gallia Lugudunensis,
revolted from Nero in March A.D. 68, L. Verginius Rufus, the
commander of the army of Upper Germany, marched against
him, and in a battle fought outside Vesontio, the German
legions annihilated the untrained Gauls opposed to them (Dio
Cass. 63. 24). Immediately afterwards the legions offered
the Empire to Verginius (Dio Cass. 63. 25), and though he
refused it, partly on the ground that the successor of the Julii
must belong to the old nobility (cf. Tac. *Hist.* 1. 52. 7: *Ver-
ginium equestri familia ignoto patre*), partly because he was a
sincere Republican (cf. his epitaph in Plin. *Ep.* 9. 19: *hic
situs est Rufus pulso qui Vindice quondam | imperium adseruit
non sibi sed patriae.* Dio Cass. 63. 25. 3: τῇ τε γὰρ γερουσίᾳ
καὶ τῷ δήμῳ προσήκειν [τὸ κράτος] ἔλεγεν), it was considered
doubtful whether he would persist in his renunciation of the
Principate to which his position as holder of one of the most
important commands in the Empire gave him a strong claim.

It must have been at this moment that No. 61 was erected by some dependent of Verginius on one of his estates, which we know were in the neighbourhood of Comum (Plinius, *Ep.* 2. 1. 8, says that one of the reasons for their friendship was that *utrique eadem regio, municipia finitima, agri etiam posses-sionesque coniunctae*). Apart from the irregularity of attri-buting a victory to a *legatus*, the formula *pro salute* is one appropriated to reigning Emperors (see Index to Wilmanns, *Exempla*, p. 677); and the whole inscription is a record of the difficulty which the army and friends of Verginius must have had in realising that he would refuse the prize that was within his grasp.

Mommsen, *Hermes*, vi. (1872) 127, xiii (1878) 90. *Provinces*, i. 82, 127.

L. Clodius Macer.

62.

B. M. C. Emp. i, Macer, 1. p. 285. Denarius.

Obverse. L. CLODIVS MACER S. C.   Head of Macer.
Reverse. PROPRAE. AFRICAE.   Representation of a galley.

63.

Cohen, i. p. 318, No. 9. Denarius.

Obverse. ROMA S. C.   Head of Roma wearing helmet.
Reverse. L. CLODI MACRI.   Representation of a trophy.

64.

Cohen, i. p. 317, No. 2. Denarius.

Obverse. L. CLODI MACRI S. C.   Female figure (Liberty) hold-ing cap of Liberty and patera.
Reverse. LEG. I. LIB. MACRIANA.   Legionary eagle and two ensigns.

65.

Cohen, i. p. 317, No. 6. Denarius. *Liberatrix* refers to Africa.

Obverse. L. CLODI MACRI LIBERATRIX S. C. Bust of Africa.
Reverse. LEG. III. LIB. AVG. Same type as No. 64.

These coins, with a few others (see Cohen, i. p. 317, and references given below), are the only monuments which we possess of the somewhat obscure attempt made by L. Clodius Macer, the Imperial legatus in Africa (Suet. *Galba*, 11), to seize the Principate on the death of Nero. There can be little doubt that his real intention was to become Emperor, but the coins show that he began by posing as a Republican, probably with a view to securing the support of the Senate. It will be noticed that all his coins, though silver, are issued in the name of that body ; that on all but one (No. 62) his name appears in the genitive, and his effigy is omitted ; and that at least one of them (No. 63) is a direct imitation of the coinage of the Republic. Moreover he calls himself *propraetor Africae* (No. 62), the regular title of the Governors of Africa before the establishment of the Empire. Tacitus mentions (*Hist.* 2. 97. 3) *legio cohortesque delectae a Clodio Macro*, and we learn from No. 64 that he called the new legion by his own name. It is uncertain whether the epithet, in the case of both legions, is *lib(era*, i. e. belonging to the Senatus Populusque Romanus and not to the Emperor, or *lib(eratrix*), as in the case of Africa (No. 65), because they were the instruments for emancipating the Roman world from Imperial rule. The first steps of Macer may be compared with those of Galba. Suet. *Galba*, 10 : *legatum se senatus ac populi R. professus est. Dein . . . e plebe quidem provinciae legiones et auxilia conscripsit super exercitum veterem.* The galley represented on No. 62 seems to imply some command of the sea, and on the reverse of two of his coins (*B.M.C. Emp.* i, Macer, 5 & n.) is the legend *Sicilia*, with the conventional

emblem of the island (the tri·skelis).   This perhaps helps to
illustrate the report that he meant to starve Rome out by
keeping back the grain-ships (Tac. *Hist.* I. 73. 2.   Plutarch,
Galba, 13).   Before this and other designs could be carried
out he was crushed (Tac. *Hist.* I. 7).

Eckhel, vi. 288-290.
L. Müller, *Numismatique de l'ancienne Afrique,* ii. 170-174.
Mommsen, *Römisches Münzwesen,* 745 and note 17.   *C. I. L.* viii. p. xx.
Cagnat, *L'Armée Romaine d'Afrique,* 149-154.

Otho.

66.

C. I. L. vi. 2051, 76-80.   Entry in the Acta Fratrum Arvalium (see Introduction, p. xvi) for March 14, A. D. 69.

Isdem cos pr. idus Mart.
vota nuncupata pro s[*al*]ute et reditu [*Vitelli*] Germanici
imp. praeeunte L. Maecio
Postumo, mag(isterio) [*Vitelli*] Germanici imp., pro-
mag(istro) Maecio Postumo, coll(egi) fratrum
Arval(ium) nomine Iov(i) b(ovem) m(arem), Iun(oni)
vacc(am), Min(ervae) vacc(am), Saluti p(ublicae)
p(opuli) R(omani) vacc(am), divo Aug(usto) b(ovem)
m(arem),
divae Aug(ustae) vacc(am), divo Claudio b(ovem)
m(arem). In coll(egio) adf(uerunt) L. Maecius
Postumus.

The Emperor, for whose safety and return these *vota* were
made on March 14, was not Vitellius but Otho, for the latter
was still in Rome at that date (Tac. *Hist.* I. 90 : *pridie idus
Martias commendata patribus republica,* &c. ; cf. id. 5 : *pro-
fectus Otho*).   His death took place on April 16 (Clinton,
Fasti Romani, and cf. Tac. *Hist.* 2. 55 : [when the news
came to Rome] *Ceriales ludi* [April 19] *ex more spectabantur*),
and the *dies imperii* of Vitellius was April 19 (*Acta, C. I. L.*

vi. 2051, l. 85, Henzen, p. 64: *ob diem imperi [Vitelli]*
Germanici imp(eratoris) quod XIII K. Mai(as) statutum est),
when he also took the place which Otho had held as *magister*
collegii. The entry therefore must have been altered to its
present form before it was engraved on the marble, some time
after the latter date. Finally, after the death of Vitellius
(Dec. 22), his name was erased. For the form in which it
appears, see p. 80.

The Invasion of Italy: A. D. 69.

67.

C. I. L. xi. 1196. The lower half of a gravestone, now in the Museum at
Parma. Probably found in or near Veleia.

IIII · MAC Ͽ

ANN · XXV ·

STIP Ͻ II ·

VEXILLÁRI

5   LEG · TRIV́M

LEG · IIII · MAC

LEG · XXI · RᴬP

LEG · XXII · PRI

P Ͻ D · S

. . . *leg(ionis)] IIII Mac(edonicae), ann(orum) XXV stip-*
(endiorum) II ; vexillari leg(ionum) trium, leg(ionis) IIII
Mac(edonicae) leg. XXI Rap(acis), leg. XXII Pri(migeniae)
p(osuerunt) d(e) s(uo).

This soldier belonged to the first of the two divisions with
which Vitellius attacked Italy in A.D. 69, that commanded
by Caecina, which took the shortest route to Italy from the
Rhine over the Great St. Bernard, and was composed, as we
see from this inscription and from Tacitus, of detachments
from the three legions which formed the army of Upper
Germany at this time (*Hist.* 1. 61. 2: *triginta milia Caecina e*

*superiore Germania ducebat, quorum robur legio unaetvicen-
sima fuit,* cf. 55. 3).   He must have fallen in one of the
unsuccessful attacks on Placentia, described in Tacitus, *Hist.*
2. 20–22.   The members of all three legions join in the
memorial as forming for the time being a single force.

Vitellius and the Senate.   Consul Perpetuus.

68.

C. I. L. vi. 929. Cf. *St. R.* ii. 1097, note 2.   The only inscription from the
city of Rome relating to Vitellius which is known. The original has disappeared.
The pedestal (probably belonging to a statue) on which it is inscribed seems to
have escaped destruction by being converted into a sepulchral urn.

A · VITELLIVS · L · F

· IMPERATOR ·

· COS · PERP ·

Suetonius, *Vitellius,* 11 : *comitia in decem annos ordinavit
seque perpetuum consulem.*   The renunciation of the. annual
Consulship by Augustus being the decisive measure which
distinguished the Principate from the Republican Magistracy
(p. 6), the action of Vitellius in restoring the arrangement of
B.C. 27 was no doubt, as Schiller suggests (*Gesch. der Kaiserzeit,* i. 381), intended to secure the support of the Senate, a
view which is confirmed by the fact that when Gaius on his
accession declared that he would be only the instrument of
the Senate's will (Dio Cass. 59. 6), that body proposed that
he should κατ' ἔτος ὑπατεύειν (l. c. 6. 5).   This attitude of
Vitellius to the Senate is illustrated by the anecdote in Tacitus, *Hist.* 2. 91. 5, and by some of the coins issued by the
Imperial Mint (cf. esp. *B. M. C. Emp.* i, Vit. 14, aureus with
SPQR on the reverse).

The inscription further illustrates the fact that Vitellius,
with a similar political intention, refused to assume the names
Augustus and Caesar (Suet. *Vit.* 8 : *cognomen Germanici
delatum ab universis cupide recepit, Augusti distulit, Caesaris*

in perpetuum recusavit. Tac. *Hist.* 2. 62. 3, but cf. 2. 90. 2, 3.
58. 5). If the view taken of this inscription be correct, the
absence of 'Germanicus' will not be surprising, referring as
that title did to the real source of his power, the German
legions (Tac. *Hist.* I. 62. 4).

For the names of Vitellius see Wilmanns, i. p. 295.

Civilis and the Imperium Galliarum.
69.

B. M. C. Emp. i, p. 308 (d) ; cp. p. cci. Denarius.

Obverse. ADSERTOR LIBERTATIS. Young male head, helmeted.
Reverse. LEGION · XV · PRIMIG · Victory crowning a military
  trophy with a helmet,

The rising of the Batavi (see p. 110) in A.D. 69 under Julius
Civilis, supported by the German tribes, and in Gaul by the
Treveri under Julius Classicus and the Lingones, reached its
climax when the camp of the Fifth and Fifteenth Legions at
Vetera surrendered to Civilis, and its garrison was annihilated
(Tac. *Hist.* iv. 60). Mr. Mattingly has suggested that No. 69
may commemorate this event. In that case the trophy
Legion(is) XV Primig(eniae) on the reverse will be explained
by the fact that, though the Legio V Alaudae was also quartered
at Vetera, the bulk of it, with its eagle, had gone to Italy
(Tac. *Hist.* i. 61, ii. 43, iii. 22) ; whereas the Fifteenth had sent
only a *vexillatio* (Tac. *Hist.* ii. 100). Hence it was the main
representative of the Roman army at Vetera. Dessau, however,
(*Geschichte der römischen Kaiserzeit*, ii, pt. 2. 387, n. 1) rejects
this interpretation, and would class No. 69 with the Spanish
and Gallic coins of A.D. 68 (*B. M. C. Emp.* i, pp. clxxxix sqq.,
288 sqq.), when allegiance to Nero had been thrown off, and it
was expected that Verginius Rufus would become Emperor.
The trophy will then refer to some unknown success of the
legion.

The *Imperium Galliarum* (Tac. *Hist.* iv. 59), which also
appears to have issued coins, with e.g. the head of *Gallia*
'defiantly national, with her native trumpet' (*B. M. C. Emp.* i,

pp. cc, 308), found no support in the country at large (Tac.
Hist. iv. 68 sqq.), and, like the rising of Civilis, quickly
collapsed in face of the overwhelming Roman forces which
were hurried to the Lower Rhine (Tac. *Hist.* iv. 68. 5).

Accession of Vespasian.   The Lex de Imperio.

70.

C. I. L. vi. 930.   On a bronze tablet now in the Capitoline Museum at Rome,
where it has been preserved since 1576.   Probably discovered in the fourteenth
century, when it was set up by Cola di Rienzi in St. John Lateran.

. . . .

foedusve cum quibus volet facere liceat, ita uti licuit divo
   Aug(usto),
Ti. Iulio Caesari Aug., Tiberioque Claudio Caesari Aug.
   Germanico ;
utique ei senatum habere, relationem facere, remittere, senatus
   consulta per relationem discessionemque facere liceat,
5   ita uti licuit divo Aug., Ti. Iulio Caesari Aug., Ti. Claudio
   Caesari
   Augusto Germanico ;
utique cum ex voluntate auctoritateve iussu mandatuve eius
   praesenteve eo senatus habebitur, omnium rerum ius
   perinde
   habeatur servetur, ac si e lege senatus edictus esset
   habereturque ;
10 utique quos magistratum potestatem imperium curationemve
   cuius rei petentes senatui populoque Romano commen-
   daverit,
   quibusque suffragationem suam dederit promiserit, eorum
   comitis quibusque extra ordinem ratio habeatur ;
utique ei fines pomerii proferre promovere, cum ex re publica
15   censebit esse, liceat ita uti licuit Ti. Claudio Caesari Aug.
   Germanico ;
utique quaecunque ex usu rei publicae maiestate[que]
   divinarum
   huma[na]rum publicarum privatarumque rerum esse

censebit, ei agere facere ius potestasque sit, ita uti divo
    Aug.,

20 Tiberioque Iulio Caesari Aug.,Tiberioque Claudio Caesari
    Aug. Germanico fuit ;

utique quibus legibus plebeive scitis scriptum fuit ne divus
    Aug.,

Tiberiusve Iulius Caesar Aug., Tiberiusque Claudius
    Caesar Aug.

Germanicus tenerentur, iis legibus plebisque scitis Imp.
    Caesar

25 Vespasianus solutus sit; quaeque ex quaque lege rogatione
    divum Aug., Tiberiumve Iulium Caesarem Aug., Tiber-
    iumve

Claudium Caes. Aug. Germanicum facere oportuit,

ea omnia imp. Caesari Vespasiano Aug. facere liceat ;

utique quae ante hanc legem rogatam acta gesta

30 decreta imperata ab imperatore Caesare Vespasiano Aug.

iussu mandatuve eius a quoque sunt, ea perinde iusta
    rataq(ue)

sint, ac si populi plebisve iussu acta essent.

Sanctio.

Si quis huiusce legis ergo adversus leges rogationes
    plebisve scita

Senatusve consulta fecit fecerit, sive, quod eum ex lege
    rogatione

plebisve scito s(enatus)ve ·c(onsulto) facere oportebit,
    non fecerit huius legis

ergo, id ei ne fraudi esto neve quit ob eam rem populo
    dare debeto,

neve cui de ea re actio neve iudicatio esto, neve quis
    de ea re apud

[*s*]e agi sinito.

This fragment is the only example which has come down
to us, of the single legislative act by which the Princeps was
constitutionally invested with the various powers which made

G 2

up the Principate. Cf. Dio Cassius, 53. 32. 6 : (Augustus) καὶ οἱ μετ᾽ αὐτὸν αὐτοκράτορες ἐν νόμῳ δή τινι τοῖς τε ἄλλοις καὶ τῇ ἐξουσίᾳ τῇ δημαρχικῇ ἐχρήσαντο. Gaius, 1. 5 : *cum ipse impe-rator per legem imperium accipiat.* Ulpian, *Dig.* 14. 1 : *cum lege regia quae de imperio eius lata est populus ei ⟨impe-rium⟩ et in eum omne suum imperium et potestatem conferat.* The existing fragment contains only the latter part of this *lex,* but it is simplest to assume that its earlier clauses con-ferred both the *imperium* and the *tribunicia potestas,* for while the passages quoted above are definite as to the single act, that act is spoken of sometimes as the *lex de imperio* (Ulpian, l. c.), sometimes as concerned with the *tribunicia potestas* (*Acta Fr. Arv.* Henzen, p. 65 [Otho, Vitellius, Domi-tian] *ob comitia tribuniciae potestatis*), according as the one or the other of the two most important elements of the Emperor's power is emphasized.

The magistrate (probably a Consul; Tac. *Ann.* 1. 13. 4. *St. R.* ii. 874, note 3) who brought the *rogatio* before the Comitia (probably the Centuriata, *St. R.* ii. 875, note 1), was of course authorised to do so by a decree of the Senate, strictly defining the terms of the proposal. Hence, while No. 70 is referred to as a *lex* (ll. 29, 34, 36), the clauses are in the form of those of a *senatus consultum* (introduced by *uti* depending on *censuerunt* : the form of a *lex* is imperative as the *Sanctio* is here), for the *lex de imperio* embodied the actual decree of the Senate. The proceedings in the Senate being practically of more importance than the formality in the Campus, the *senatus consultum* is often the only act mentioned (Tac. *Hist.* 1. 47. 2 : *adcurrunt patres ; decernitur Othoni tribunicia potestas et nomen Augusti et omnes principum honores. Vita Probi,* 12. 8 : *decerno igitur p. c. votis om-nium concinentibus nomen imperatorium, nomen Caesareanum, nomen Augustum, addo proconsulare imperium, patris patriae reverentiam, pontificatum maximum, ius tertiae relationis, tribu-niciam potestatem. Post haec adclamatum est: 'omnes, omnes').*

The frequent references to the precedents of former *leges de imperio* (Nero is omitted as *damnatae memoriae*, and Gaius as practically though not formally so treated, Dio Cass. 60. 4. 5) emphásize the fact that, while the general object of the measure was to place the Emperor designate in the position held by Augustus after B.C. 23, that position was only the result of the concentration in one hand of a number of powers which might be varied or enlarged according to circumstances. The only positive additions to the powers held by Augustus, are the *ius proferendi pomerii* (l. 14), and possibly the unlimited right of *commendatio* (!. 10).

ll. 1, 2. Strabo, 17. 3. 25, p. 840: (Augustus) πολέμου καὶ εἰρήνης κατέστη κύριος διὰ βίου. Dio Cass. 53. 17. 5: πολέμους τε ἀναιρεῖσθαι καὶ εἰρήνην σπένδεσθαι. Cf. Suet. *Cl.* 25: *cum regibus foedus in foro icit porca caesa ac vetere fetialium praefatione adhibita.*

ll. 3–9. The next two clauses refer to the Emperor's rights with regard to meetings and business of the Senate, apart from those which he possessed by virtue of his *tribunicia potestas.* Augustus was empowered (Dio Cass. 53. 32. 5) χρηματίζειν περὶ ἑνός τινος ὅτου ἂν ἐθελήσῃ καθ᾿ ἑκάστην βουλήν, κἂν μὴ ὑπατεύῃ (*relationem facere*), and (Dio Cass. 54. 3. 3) τὴν βουλὴν ἀθροίζειν ὁσάκις ἂν ἐθελήσῃ (*senatum habere*). The reasons which made these special powers necessary, have been explained above, p. 8. *Relationem remittere* is explained by Tacitus, *Ann.* 3. 10: *Fulcinius Trio Pisonem apud consules postulavit . . . petitum est a principe cognitionem exciperet . . . (Tiberius) integram causam ad senatum remittit* (*St. R.* ii. 900). *Per relationem discessionemque* does not refer to two methods of obtaining the decision of the Senate, but, as the copula shows, to one only, that *per discessionem*; *per relationem* being inserted as the necessary preliminary to every decree of the Senate, whether there were a *perrogatio sententiarum* or not (*St. R.* iii. 983, note 4).

ll. 10–13. From the beginning the Emperors practically

controlled the elections to all magistracies, either by their right *commendare candidatos sine repulsa et ambitu designandos* (Tac. *Ann.* 1. 15. 2), or by the use they made of their power to receive the names of candidates (e. g. Tac. *Ann.* 1. 14. 6 : *candidatos praeturae duodecim nominavit*). It will be noticed that the present clause, dealing with the former right, that of *commendatio*, is quite unlimited, and that it contains no reference to precedents. The earlier Emperors, whatever their powers may have been, certainly only made a restricted use of the right (*St. R.* ii. 923, no instances in case of the Consulship. For the other magistracies, cf. Tac. *Ann.* 1. 15. 2 : *moderante Tiberio ne plures quam quattuor candidatos commendaret*), whereas from the time of Nero onwards we find even the Consuls appointed in this way (Tac. *Hist.* 1. 77. 2 : [*Otho*] *proximos menses Verginio destinat . . . iungitur Verginio Pompeius Vopiscus . . . ceteri consulatus ex destinatione Neronis aut Galbae mansere*). It is therefore possible that the unlimited power of *commendatio* here given to Vespasian may date only from the reign of Nero (*St. R.* ii. 924). Illusory as was the effect of such a renunciation of privilege, it must be remembered that even after Vespasian the Emperors did not make full use of the unlimited right, as the title *candidatus Caesaris* shows.

ll. 14–16. See No. 73. The omission of the name of Augustus here, and the silence of the Ancyran Monument are conclusive against Tacitus, *Ann.* 12. 23. 5, and Dio Cass. 55. 6. 6. *St. R.* ii. 1072.

ll. 17–21. Ulpian, *Dig.* 1. 4. 1 : *quod principi placuit legis habet vigorem . . . quodcumque igitur imperator per epistulam et subscriptionem statuit vel cognoscens decrevit vel de plano interlocutus est vel edicto praecepit legem esse constat: haec sunt quas vulgo constitutiones appellamus.* The *iusiurandum in acta*, not only those of the reigning Princeps, but also those of his predecessors (except those *damnatae memoriae*), is a necessary consequence of this power. *St. R.* ii. 909.

ll. 22–28. The Emperor is not set above the law, but by exception exempted from its operation in particular cases. Hence we find Emperors applying to the Senate for exemptions in cases not covered by this clause, cf. Dio Cass. 56. 32, 59. 15. Later the Emperor was regarded as able to dispense himself in every case (*St. R.* ii. 751).

ll. 29–32. This retrospective ratification brings out the distinction between the designation of the Imperator by acclamation of the Senate or army, and his legal investiture with the powers of the Principate. The former authorised him in a sense to act as Emperor, and Vespasian dated his accession from it (Suet. *Vesp.* 6 : *Kl. Iul. qui principatus dies in posterum observatus est*). The ratification was specially necessary in the present case when some time had elapsed .since the designation.

Prof. Pelham, *Journal of Philology*, xvii. 45–51. According to the other authorities the *imperium* and the *tribunicia potestas* were conferred by separate acts, the additional powers of No. 70 forming part of the *lex de tribunicia potestate* (Mommsen, *Staatsrecht*, ii. 874–881 ; Willems, *Droit Public Romain*, 5th ed. 422, 426), and the *imperium* being given by the army or Senate.

II. ROME AND ITALY.
Claudius and the Water Supply of Rome.
71.

C. I. L. vi. 1256. Above the two arches (afterwards converted into the Porta Maggiore) which carried the Aqua Claudia and the Anio Novus over the fork formed by the Via Labicana and Via Praenestina. Below this inscription are two others referring to restorations by Vespasian and Titus.

TI · CLAVDIVS · DRVSI · F · CAISAR · AVGVSTVS · GER-
    MANICVS · PONTIF · MAXIM
TRIBVNICIA · POTESTATE · $\overline{\mathrm{XII}}$ · COS · $\overline{\mathrm{V}}$ · IMPERATOR ·
    XXVII · PATER · PATRIAE
AQVAS · CLAVDIAM · EX FONTIBVS · QVI · VOCABANTVR ·
    CAERVLEVS · ET ·, CVRTIVS · A MILLIARIO · XXXXV
ITEM · ANIENEM · NOVAM · A MILLIARIO · LXII · SVA ·
    IMPENSA · IN VRBEM · PERDVCENDAS · CVRAVIT

72.

C. I. L. vi. 1252.   Above an arch of the aqueduct, which stands behind a house in the Via del Nazzareno, not far from the Fountain of Trevi the modern terminus of the Aqua Virgo.

TI · CLAVDIVS · DRVSI · F · CAESAR · AVGVSTVS · GER-
  MANICVS

PONTIFEX · MAXIM · TRIB · POTEST · V̄ · IMP · X̄Ī · P ·
  P · COS · DESIG · ĪĪĪĪ

ARCVS · DVCTVS · AQVAE · VIRGINIS · DISTVRBATÓS · PER ·
  C · CAESAREM

A FVNDAMENTIS · NOVÓS · FECIT · AC · RESTITVIT

Claudius, following the example of Augustus, devoted considerable attention to the condition of Rome (Suet. *Cl.* 18 : *urbis curam sollicitissime semper egit*), and particularly to the completion of its water supply.   In A.D. 52 two aqueducts which had been begun by Gaius in A.D. 38, were finished under the names of the Aqua Claudia and the Anio Novus (No. 71, cf. Frontinus, *de Aq.* 13.   Tac. *Ann.* 11. 13. 2.   Suet. *Cl.* 20).   Both came from the Sabine mountains to the East of Rome, and the former from near the source of the Aqua Marcia which was considered to have the best water of all (hence Frontinus, *de Aq.* 13 : *haec bonitate proxima est Marciae.*   Cf. 14 : [the Claudia besides the springs mentioned in No. 71] *accipit et eum fontem qui vocatur Albudinus, tantae bonitatis ut Marciae quoque adiutorio quotiens opus est ita sufficiat ut adiectus ei nihil ex qualitate eius mutet.*)   For the magnificent scale on which the Claudia was carried out see Pliny, *H. N.* 36. 122.

The Aqua Virgo restored by Claudius in A.D. 46 (No. 72. *C. I. L.* vi. 1254 a boundary stone of the same restoration is dated A.D. 44–45), entered Rome on the North, and was one of the works of Agrippa (see p. 28).   The reference to Gaius (l. 3) is characteristic and may be compared with the reflection on Tiberius in No. 79. 11, and the edict in Josephus (*Ant.* 19. 5. 2) there quoted.

Such important additions to the system of Roman aqueducts required a corresponding increase in the establishments connected with them. Hitherto the slaves employed belonged to the State (*familia publica*) and the expenses connected with their maintenance were paid through the Aerarium (Frontin. 118), an arrangement which dated from the death of Agrippa. When Claudius completed his new aqueducts he set apart for their service a number of his own slaves (*familia Caesaris*), who were of course supported by the Emperor's purse (Frontin. 118). The two *familiae* were kept distinct and continued to exist side by side. Frontin. *de Aq.* 116 : *familiae sunt duae, altera publica, altera Caesaris. Publica est antiquior ; quam ab Agrippa relictam Augusto et ab eo publicatam diximus* [98] : *habet homines circiter ducentos quadraginta. Caesaris familiae numerus est quadringentorum sexaginta ; quam Claudius cum aquas in urbem perduceret constituit. Utraque autem familia in aliquot ministeriorum species diducitur.* Of great importance for the Imperial control of the whole system was the appointment at the same time of a *procurator aquarum* (Frontin. *de Aq.* 105 : *libertum Caesaris . . . procuratorem primus Ti. Claudius videtur admovisse postquam Anienem Novum et Claudiam induxit*).

R. Lanciani, *Comentarii di Frontino. Atti d. Accad. dei Lincei*, ser. 3. vol. 4, (1880), 215 sqq. and esp. 539.

Hirschfeld, *Verwaltungsbeamten*, 275 sqq.

Claudius and the Pomerium.

73.

C. I. L. vi. 1231. One of four known examples of the cippi which marked out the Pomerium of Claudius. This one is built into the wall of a house in the Via di S. Lucia near the place where it was discovered. The date is A. D. 49. For the official adoption of the Digamma and other new letters by Claudius in A. D. 47, see Tacitus, *Ann.* 11. 14. 5.

TI · CLAVDIVS
DRVSI · F · CAISAR
AVG · GERMANICVS

PONT · MAX · TRIB · POT

5   VIIII · IMP · X̅V̅I̅ · COS · I̅I̅I̅I̅

CENSOR · P · P

AVCTI̅S · POPVLI · ROMANI

FI̅NIBVS · POMERIVM

AMPLIAꓯIT · TERMINAꓯITQ

Claudius, who had a special taste for constitutional antiquities, performed in A.D. 49 (probably in connection with his Census of A.D. 47) the act of enlarging the ideal boundary of the City known as the Pomerium (Tac. *Ann.* 12. 23. 4). The right to do this was traditionally one of the prerogatives of the kings, and under the Republic the practice was suspended until the dictatorship of Sulla. Claudius apparently was empowered to enlarge the Pomerium by a special enactment (No. 70. 14 : *utique ei fines pomerii proferre ... liceat ita uti licuit Tiberio Claudio Caesari Augusto Germanico*) which may, as Detlefsen suggests (*Hermes*, xxi. 505), have been intended to settle the constitutional question which had arisen by the time of Claudius as to the conditions under which the act could be performed. Cf. the contemporary reference of Seneca (*de Brev. Vit.* 13. 8) : *Sullam ultimum Romanorum protulisse pomerium quod nunquam provinciali sed Italico agro adquisito proferre moris apud antiquos fuit.* There is nothing to tell us in which sense the controversy was decided by Claudius, but the formula on his cippi, *auctis populi Romani finibus*, is more in accordance with the theory that existed in the last century of the Republic (Gellius, 13. 14. 3 : *habebat autem ius proferendi pomerii qui populum Romanum agro de hostibus capto auxerat*) than statements such as that of Tacitus (*Ann.* 12. 23. 4) : *iis qui protulere imperium etiam terminos urbis propagare datur* (cf. *Vita Aureliani*, 21. 10 : *pomerio autem neminem principum licet addere nisi eum qui agri barbarici aliqua parte Romanam rempublicam locupletaverit*). Moreover Detlefsen has shown that it is possible to prove an actual increase of the *ager Italicus* and of the number of citizens in Italy under every one of the Emperors to whom an extension of the Pomerium is ascribed (l. c. 561), and therefore Claudius may have based his claim as much e. g. on the grant of Roman citizenship to the Anauni (see No. 79) as on the conquest of Britain.

It was not till this enlargement of the Pomerium by Claudius that the Aventine was included within the legal boundary of the city (Gellius, 13. 14), a proof that it was only in the very earliest times that the Pomerium coincided with the actual wall, for that of Servius took in the Aventine. As might have been expected the Campus Martius for constitutional reasons (connected e. g. with the Triumph and N. B. the presence there of the Imperial Mausoleum) still remained outside the *fines urbani auspicii* (Gell. l. c.), for one of the cippi of Hadrian's restoration has been found between it and the city proper.

D. Detlefsen, *Das Pomerium Roms und die Grenzen Italiens. Hermes,* xxi. (1886), 497.

O. Richter, *Topographie von Rom* (in Iwan Müller's *Handbuch,* vol. 3, 2nd ed., 64–66.

Construction of the Portus Romanus.

74.

C. I. L. xiv. 85. On a slab of marble found among the ruins of the Portus Romanus, where it still remains. The letters were originally of bronze. The date is A. D. 46.

TI · CLAVDIVS · DRVSI · F · CAESAR
AVG · GERMANICVS · PONTIF · MAX
TRIB · POTEST · V̄Ī · COS · DESIGN · ĪĪĪĪ · IMP · X̄ĪĪ · P · P
FOSSIS · DVCTIS · A · TIBERI · OPERIS · PORTV*s*
5   CAVSSÁ · EMISSISQVE · INMARE · VRBEM
INVNDATIONIS · PERICVLO · LIBERAVIT

75·

C. I. L. xiv. 163. On a circular bronze plate intended to be fastened to a wall.
Whether found at Ostia is not known.   Now in the Museum at Berlin.

CLAVDI

OPTATI

AVG · L

PROC · PORTVS

OSTIESIS

To Claudius belongs the credit of overcoming, in face of the
opposition of his own engineers (Dio Cass. 60. 11. 3), the ob-
stacles which had deterred Julius Caesar from carrying out
the design of giving Rome a sea-harbour (Suet. *Cl.* 20).   The
principal reason for its construction was the necessity of providing for the safety of the grain ships on which Rome depended for its food supply (Dio Cass. 60. 11 : [A.D. 142] λιμοῦ
τε ἰσχυροῦ γενομένου, οὐ μόνον τῆς ἐν τῷ τότε παρόντι ἀφθονίας τῶν
τροφῶν ἀλλὰ καὶ τῆς ἐς πάντα τὸν μετὰ ταῦτα αἰῶνα πρόνοιαν
ἐποιήσατο . . . 3 : τοῦτ' οὖν συνιδὼν λιμένα τε κατασκευάσαι ἐπε-
χείρησεν).   Previously they were unloaded either at Puteoli,
or in the open sea outside Ostia (Strabo, 5. 3. 5, p. 231 : Ὦστια
πόλις ἀλίμενος . . . παρακινδύνως μὲν οὖν ὁρμίζονται μετέωρα ἐν τῷ
σάλῳ τὰ ναυκλήρια, τὸ μέντοι λυσιτελὲς νικᾷ· καὶ γὰρ ἡ τῶν ὑπηρε-
τικῶν σκαφῶν εὐπορία τῶν ἐκδεχομένων τὰ φορτία καὶ ἀντιφορτι-
ζόντων ταχὺν ποιεῖ τὸν ἀπόπλουν, πρὶν ἢ τοῦ ποταμοῦ ἅψασθαι).

For descriptions of the harbour and its construction see Dio
Cassius, 60. 11. 4.   Pliny, *H. N.* 16. 201.   Prof. Mayor on
Juvenal, 12. 75, and cf. the references given below at the end
of the section.

The work was undertaken by Claudius in the second year
of his reign (Dio Cass. l. c.), and No. 74 shows that it was
still in progress in A.D. 46, but the undated coins of Nero
with the legend : *Port(us) Ost(iensis) Augusti* and a representation of the harbour) Eckhel, vi. 276. *B. M. C. Emp.* i, Nero,
130–135) mean that it was completed by his successor.   It was

thenceforward known as the Portus Augusti, a title which has
no reference to any supposed share of Augustus in the design
(*C. I. L.* xiv. p. 6, note 2), but was probably chosen by Nero
or his subordinates (as suggested in *C. I. L.* xiv. p. 6, note 4)
in order to deprive Claudius of the honour of giving his name
to the work. The new harbour was far from being a safe
anchorage in all weathers, for in A.D. 62 we hear of ships being
lost *portu in ipso* (Tac. *Ann.* 15. 18. 3), and the inner harbour
constructed by Trajan was intended to remedy this defect. The
canal which connected the basin with the Tiber also provided
a new outlet for the stream, the flow of which was retarded
by the sand-choked mouth at Ostia (Strabo, l. c.), and thereby
reduced the probability of inundations in Rome (No. 74. 6).

Claudius paid great attention to the food supply of the
capital (Suet. 18 : *annonae curam sollicitissime egit*), and the
measures he took for securing it from the accidents of winds
and waves were accompanied by various administrative reforms. Before his time the grain trade of Ostia had been
under the charge of the *quaestor Ostiensis* (Velleius, 2. 94. 3:
[*Tiberius Claudius Nero*] *quaestor . . . maximam difficultatem
annonae ac rei frumentariae inopiam ita Ostiae atque in urbe
mandatu vitrici moderatus est ut &c.*). The regulation of the
harbour was now put in the hands of an Imperial Procurator
(No. 75, a *libertus* apparently of Claudius), who later was
replaced by an official of higher standing, an equestrian *procurator annonae* (e.g. *C. I. L.* xiv. 161 : *Q. Calpurnio C. f(ilio)
Quir(ina) (tribu) Modesto, proc(uratori) Alpium, proc(uratori)
Ostiae ad annon(am), proc(uratori) Lucaniae, corpus mercatorum
frumentariorum, &c.*). Both of course would be subordinate
to the head of the department, the *praefectus annonae* at
Rome (*St. R.* ii. 1043).

Introduction to Inscriptions of Ostia by H. Dessau in *C. I. L.* xiv. 6–9.

R. Lanciani, *Ricerche Topografiche sulla Città di Porto : Annali dell' Instituto
di Corr. Arch.* 1868, 144.

R. Lanciani, *Ancient Rome*, 238–247.

Hirschfeld, *Verwaltungsbeamten*, 246–251.

Increase of the Guards under Claudius.

76.

C. I. L. v. 7003. On the pedestal of a statue erected by the colony of Augusta Taurinorum (Turin) to a fellow townsman (the citizens belonged to the *tribus Stellatina*, cf l. 2) who held the dignity of *patronus coloniae*. Now in the Museum at Turin. l. 12: *d*(*ecurionum*) *d*(*ecreto*).

C · GAVIO · L · F

STEL · SILVÁNO

*p*RIMIPILÁRI · LEG · VIII · AVG

*t*RIBVNO · COH · II · VIGILVM

5   *t*RIBVNO · COH · XIII · VRBAN

*tr*IBVNO · COH · XII · PRAETOR

*d*ONIS · DÓNÁTO · A · DIVO · CLAVD

BELLÓ · BRITANNICO

*to*RQVIBVS · ARMILLIS · PHALERIS

10   CORÓNÁ . ÁVREÁ

p A T R O N O · C O L O N

D   ↻   d

Under Augustus and Tiberius a force of twelve cohorts numbered consecutively, 1-9 being the *cohortes praetoriae*, 10-12 the *cohortes urbanae*, was stationed at Rome (Tac. *Ann.* 4. 5. 5 : *quamquam insideret urbem proprius miles, tres urbanae, novem praetoriae cohortes*). But there are a number of inscriptions—mainly epitaphs from the city of Rome — of officers and men of praetorian cohorts numbered eleven and twelve. At some time therefore the Guards must have been increased by three new cohorts. We know that Vitellius raised the number of cohorts to sixteen in A. D. 69 (Tac. *Hist.* 2. 93. 3), but No. 76 shows that the cohort to which Gavius Silvanus who was put to death by Nero for his share in Piso's conspiracy in A.D. 65 (Tac. *Ann.* 15. 50. 3, 71. 4), belonged was the twelfth. The change had therefore been made at least as early as the reign of Nero. As there is no reference to it in the books of Tacitus which we possess, and as it is difficult to suppose that he would have passed it over, it is not unlikely that the addition was made in the period covered by the lacuna in the Annals (death of Tiberius—A. D. 47). In that case it would not be easy to find a more appropriate occasion than the accession of Claudius, the first Emperor who owed his throne to the Guards. To strengthen the force would be at once to reward it for its services by increasing its power and prestige, and at the same time to ensure the efficiency of the means to which the Imperial government immediately owed its existence, and on which it ultimately relied for its continuance in power.

At the same time apparently the number of *cohortes urbanae* was raised to nine (cf. esp. *C. I. L.* xi. 395), i. e. in addition to the three original cohorts and the thirteenth which probably existed as early as Augustus, five new ones were enrolled.

C. Gavius Silvanus joined the army invading Britain in A. D. 43 with a detachment of the Eighth Legion to which there is another reference in the inscription (*D.* 967. Suasa in Umbria) *L. Coiedio L. f. Ani. Candido, tr. mil. leg. VIII Aug. &c. Hunc Ti. Cl(audius) Caes. Aug. Germ. revers(um) ex castr(is) don(is) mil(itaribus) don(avit) &c.*

Mommsen, *Hermes*, xiv. (1879), 25; xvi. (1881), 643.

The Guards under Vitellius.

77.

C. I. L. vi. 2725. Found on the Via Nomentana near Rome. Now in the Vatican. Moderatus must have entered the Sixteenth Legion in A.D. 59 or 60. After coming to Italy and serving for eight years in the Guards (A.D. 69-77) he entered the corps of *evocati Augusti* who were generally selected from the Praetorians for employment in various civil functions (but cf. Tac. *Ann.* 2. 68. 3) under the immediate direction of the Praefectus Praetorio. Moderatus seems to have been architect of one of the Imperial armouries (the inscription is flanked by representations of a carpenter's rule and square), i. e. perhaps he superintended its internal arrangements. He remained in the corps twenty-three years, and must have died at the age of about sixty under Trajan, in A. D.

99 or 100.   For the Evocati see Mommsen in *Eph. Epigr.* v. p. 142, and art.
Exercitus in Smith's Dict. of Antiquities, 3rd ed. p. 792.

C · VEDENNIVS · C · F
QVI · MODERATVS · AN̅Io
MILIT · IN · LEG · X̅V̅I̅ · GAL · A · X
TRANLAT · IN · COH · I̅X̅ PR
5   IN QVA · MILIT · ANN · VIII
MISSVS · HONESTA · MISSION
REVOC · AB · IMP · FACT · EVOC · AVG
ARCITECT · ARMAMENT · IMP
EVOC · ANN · XXIII
10   DONIS · MILITARIB · DONAT
BIS · AB · DIVO · VESP · ET
IMP · DOMITIANO · AVG · GERM
. . . .

C. Vedennius C. f. Qui(rina) (tribu) Moderatus, (domo)
Antio, milit(avit) in leg(ione) XVI Gal(lica) a(nnis) X, tran(s)-
lat(us) in coh(ortem) IX pr(aetoriam), in qua milit(avit) ann(is)
VIII, missus honesta mission(e), revoc(atus) ab imp(eratore),
fact(us) evoc(atus) Aug(usti), arcitect(us) armament(arii) im-
p(eratoris),evoc(atus) ann(is) XXIII, donis militarib(us) donat(us)
bis ab divo Vesp(asiano) et imp(eratore) Domitiano Aug(usto)
Germ(anico) . . . . . .

On the foundation of the Principate Augustus reconstituted
the Praetorian cohorts, which under the Triumvirate had
been selected from the legions (Appian, *B. C.* 5. 3: after Philippi
Antonius and Octavianus ἀφίεσαν τῆς στρατείας τοὺς ἐντελῆ
χρόνον ἐστρατευμένους χωρὶς ὀκτακισχιλίων οὓς δεηθέντας ἔτι στρα-
τεύεσθαι σφίσιν ἀποδεξάμενοι διείλοντο καὶ συνελόχισαν ἐς στρα-
τηγίδας τάξεις.   Cf. the coins of Antonius with *Chortium prae-*
toriarum and a representation of a legionary eagle. Eckhel, vi.
52. *B. M. C. Rep.* ii, p. 526).   Henceforward, as being more in
accordance with the *restituta respublica* (p. 4), the Guards of
the Imperator were to be kept distinct from the legions and
to be recruited separately (Tac. *Ann.* 4. 5. 5 : *novem praetoriae*
cohortes Etruria ferme Umbriaque delectae aut vetere Latio et

coloniis antiquitus Romanis). But when Vitellius was made
Emperor by the legions of the Rhine army, it was not unnatural that, relying as he did on those legions for the maintenance of his position, he should get rid of the existing
Praetorian cohorts and form new ones out of his own followers.
We know from Tacitus that he took the first step (*Hist.* 2. 67:
*proximus Vitellio e praetoriis cohortibus metus erat. separati
primum, deinde addito honestae missionis lenimento arma ad
tribunos suos deferebant*), and that when he enrolled the new
cohorts he took the opportunity of increasing their number
(*Hist.* 2. 93: *sedecim praetoriae quattuor urbanae cohortes
scribebantur quis singula milia inessent*). No. 77 shows that
the new Guard was raised from the German legions. The
Sixteenth Legion formed part of the army of Lower Germany
in A. D. 69 (Tac. *Hist.* 1. 55. 2) and marched to Italy under the
command of Valens. Cf. *Hist.* 2. 93. 3: *sedecim praetoriae . . .
cohortes scribebantur . . . plus in eo delectu Valens audebat . . .
omnisque inferioris Germaniae miles Valentem adsectabatur*).
With the fall of Vitellius his Guards were ordered to be discharged, but there were difficulties in the way of carrying out
such a measure rigorously, and it is quite consistent with the
narrative of Tacitus (*Hist.* 4. 46) that Moderatus should have
remained in the service for eight years after the accession of
Vespasian.

Mommsen, *Die Gardetruppen der römischen Republik und der Kaiserzeit. Hermes,*
xiv. (1879), 25, and esp. 32 note.

The Italian Fleet under Claudius.

78.

C. I. L. iii. p. 844, x. 769. Found at Stabiae. Now in the Museum at Naples.
The date is Dec. 11, A. D. 52. For the Diplomata Militaria see Introduction,
p. xvi.

(*a*)　　Ti. Claudius Caesar Aug. Germanicus,
　　　　pontifex maxim., trib. pot. XII, imp. XXVII,
　　　　pater patriae, censor, cos. V,

H

trierarchis et remigibus qui militave-
5   runt in classe quae est Miseni, sub Ti.
Iulio Aug(usti) lib(erto) Optato, et sunt dimissi
honesta missione, quorum nomina subscripta sunt, ipsis liberis posterisque
eorum civitatem dedit et conubium
10   cum uxoribus quas tunc habuissent
cum est civitas iis data, aut, siqui
caelibes essent, cum iis quas postea
duxissent dum taxat singuli singulas.
        a. d. iii idus Decembr.
15   Fausto Cornelio Sulla Felice,
L. Salvidieno Rufo Salviano, cos.
            gregali
Spartico Diuzeni f. Dipscurto Besso.
Descriptum et recognitum ex tabula aenea
20   quae fixa est Romae in Capitolio aedis
Fidei populi Romani parte dexteriore.

(*b*)	L. Mesti L. f.		Aem(ilia) (tribu) Prisci, Dyrrachini.
	L. Nutri		Venusti, Dyrrachini.
	C. Durrachini		Anthi, Dyrrachini.
	C. Sabini	(*Seals of the witnesses.*)	Nedymi, Dyrrachini.
	C. Corneli		Ampliati, Dyrrachini.
	T. Pomponi		Epaphroditi, Dyrrachini.
	N(umeri) Mini Hylae,		Thessalonicensis.

The Italian fleet was established by Augustus in the form
of two squadrons, the stations of which were at Ravenna and

Misenum (Suet. *Aug.* 49 : *classem Miseni et alteram Ravennac ad tutelam Superi et Inferi maris conlocavit*). Under him and his immediate successors it was manned by Imperial slaves and freedmen (e. g. *C. I. L.* ix. 41 : *Malchio Caesaris trierarchus*), but by the time of Claudius, as No. 78 shows, and probably owing to a reorganisation effected by him, free-born subjects of the Empire (*peregrini*) coming mainly from the provinces of the eastern Mediterranean had been admitted to the service. The command held by an Imperial freedman may be an arrangement peculiar to the squadron at Misenum (cf. Tac. *Ann.* 14. 3. 5 : [A. D. 59] *Anicetus libertus classi apud Misenum praefectus*), and perhaps to be explained by its immediate relation to the Emperor as his personal guard when on the coast of Campania (hence both fleets were known at a later date as *classes praetoriae*). By A. D. 56 we hear of the fleet at Ravenna being commanded by an *eques* (Tac. *Ann.* 13. 30. 2 : *Clodius Quirinalis praefectus remigum qui Ravennae haberentur.* Cf. *C. I. L.* v. 533= *D.* 2702 where his career is given), and after the time of Vespasian this is the rule for both.

Mommsen, *Hermes*, xvi. (1881), 463.

E. Ferrero, *Ordinamente delle Armate Romane.* Turin, 1878.

Romanisation of the Alpine Tribes. The Civitas given to the Anauni : A. D. 46.

79.

C. I. L. v. 5050. On a bronze tablet found in 1869 at Cles in the Val di Non (Anauni). Now at Trient. The date is March 15, A. D. 46. In the text as given below the somewhat numerous errors of the original have been corrected. In l. 33 *collecti* is for *allecti*.

M. Iunio Silano Q. Sulpicio Camerino cos.

    idibus Martis Bais in praetorio edictum

Ti. Claudi Caesaris Augusti Germanici propositum fuit id

    quod infra scriptum est.

5 Ti. Claudius Caesar Augustus Germanicus, pont.

    maxim., trib. potest., VI imp. XI, p. p., cos. designatus

    IIII, dicit :

Cum ex veteribus controversis pendentibus aliquamdiu etiam
  temporibus Ti. Caesaris patrui mei, ad quas ordinandas
  Pinarium Apollinarem miserat, quae tantum modo
10   inter Comenses essent, quantum memoria refero, et
  Bergaleos, isque primum apsentia pertinaci patrui mei,
  deinde etiam Gai principatu quod ab eo non exigebatur
  referre, non stulte quidem, neglexserit, et posteac
  detulerit Camurius Statutus ad me agros plerósque
15   et saltus mei iuris esse : in rem praesentem misi
  Plantam Iulium amicum et comitem meum qui
  cum, adhibitis procuratoribus meis quique in alia
  regione quique in vicinia erant, summa cura inqui-
  sierit et cognoverit, cetera quidem ut mihi demons-
20   trata commentario facto ab ipso sunt, statuat pronun-
  tietque ipsi permitto.
Quod ad condicionem Anaunorum et Tulliassium et Sinduno-
  rum pertinet, quorum partem delator adtributam Tridentinis, partem ne adtributam quidem arguisse dicitur,
25   tam et si animadverto non nimium firmam id genus hominum habere civitatis Romanae originem : tamen cum longa
  usurpatione in possessionem eius fuisse dicatur et ita
    permix-
    tum cum Tridentinis ut diduci ab is sine gravi splendidi
    municipi
    iniuria non possit, patior eos in eo iure, in quo esse se
    existima-
30   verunt, permanere benificio meo, eo quidem libentius quod
  plerique ex eo genere hominum etiam militare in praetorio
  meo dicuntur, quidam vero ordines quoque duxisse,
  non nulli collecti in decurias Romae res iudicare.
Quod benificium is ita tribuo ut quaecumque tanquam
35   cives Romani gesserunt egeruntque aut inter se aut cum
  Tridentinis alisve, rata esse iubeam, nominaque ea
  quae habuerunt antea tanquam cives Romani, ita habere
    is permittam.

It is the latter portion of this inscription (l. 22 : *quod ad condicionem Anaunorum, &c.*) which is most important for historical purposes, but it is necessary to explain the circumstances under which the whole edict was issued. It has been shown above (p. 38) how the principle of *attributio* was applied to certain of the Alpine tribes partly in B. C. 89, partly by Augustus. Among those so attached to neighbouring *municipia* at the earlier date (they are not included in the list of the Tropaea Alpium, No. 31, cf. Plin. *H. N.* 3. 138) were the tribes mentioned in the present document, and it appears that the civilizing effects of the system were very marked in their case. While it was the rule that the *attributi* should be a grade below the governing *municipium* in political rights (hence after the Transpadane towns received Roman citizenship from Caesar the Anauni, &c., probably became *iuris Latini*), the social connection of these tribes with Tridentum became so close that the legal distinction between them became practically obsolete, and individuals at least, acted as if the *loca attributa* to which they belonged formed part of the *territorium* of Tridentum and they themselves were citizens of the *municipium* and consequently shared its full political privileges (l. 31). This process of informal unification had an interest for the department of the Fiscus, for though the *attributi* paid their local rates to the *municipium* (cf. *C. I. L.* v. 532. 2. 12 = *D.* 6680 : [of the Carni and Catali in relation to Tergeste] *qui erant tantum in. reditu pecuniario*) and were therefore outside its sphere, it seems that portions of these tribes had never been included in the original *attributio* (l. 24) and consequently, as conquered territory, formed part of the domain of Caesar and could be dealt with by the Imperial officials. It was important therefore in view of the general effacement of the original legal and territorial distinctions in these parts, to ascertain clearly what belonged to the *municipia* and what to Caesar. In the case of Comum an investigation of the kind had been begun as far back as Tiberius (l. 7), but under Claudius the question was raised in the interest of the Fiscus by an information laid by Camurius Statutus (ll. 14, 23), and an official inquiry directed to be held by a special commissioner assisted by the Procurators of the Imperial domains in North Italy (ll. 16–18 the *procurator Raetiae* is probably included. Mommsen, l. c. inf.). Of the details of the decision to which they came we are not informed (ll. 18–21).

But in the course of the investigation of the question between the Fiscus and the *municipium*, it had been necessary to inquire into the status of the tribes dependent on Tridentum, and the result had been to affirm the almost forgotten fact that they were *attributi* and not *cives municipii*. That fact did not affect their independence of the Fiscus, which could only make good its claims in the case of those proved to be not *attributi* at all ; but it still remained a question how the persons who had acted on the false assumption that they were citizens of Tridentum, were to be treated. Claudius answers this by ratifying the assumed status and thereby abolishing the political consequences of the *attributio*. The system therefore has here produced its full result, and the Anauni who began their connection with Rome as a conquered tribe with the rights of *peregrini*, have become, first by popular recognition, and then in the eye of the law, full Roman citizens.

In the document itself the following points may be noticed. The frequent use of the *edictum* by Claudius is noticed by Suetonius (*Cl.* 16 : *uno die XX edicta proposuit*). No. 82 is another instance.

l. 2. *praetorium* is correctly used of any residence of the Imperator, and hence it comes to mean the quarters of the Guards who are always in attendance on him (l. 31). But the use of the name here for the Imperial Villa at Baiae is certainly the beginning of the transition to its more general meaning which was established before the end of the century (Statius, *Silv.* 1. 3. 25). Cf. also No. 92. 10.

ll. 11, 12. For similar reflections on his predecessors, cf. No.
72, and esp. in the letter to the *praefectus Aegypti* about the
Jews given by Josephus (*Ant.* 19. 5. 2) : ἐπὶ τῶν Γαΐου Καίσαρος
χρόνων τοῦ διὰ τὴν πολλὴν ἀπόνοιαν καὶ παραφροσύνην . . . ταπεινώ-
σαντος αὐτούς.

l. 16. *Amicus* and *comes* are both technical expressions, the
former implying merely the right of access to the presence
of the Emperor, while the *comes* is an *amicus* selected to
accompany the Emperor when he leaves Italy and receiving
a fixed *viaticum* while his attendance lasts.   (Suet. *Tib.* 46).
Julius Planta had probably acted in this capacity during the
expedition of Claudius to Britain (*St. R.* ii. 834–836).

l. 31. The fact that natives of the districts round Tridentum served in the Guards shows that by the time of Claudius
they were no longer solely recruited from the places mentioned in Tacitus, *Ann.* 4. 5. 5. Henceforward the Guards were
distinguished by being a force of Italians.   (For later extensions, cf. Dio Cass. 74. 2. 4).   For instances of Praetorians
from the Anauni, cf. *C. I. L.* v. 5071, 5072.

l. 33. Just as with the service in the Guards, so the qualifi-
cation for appearing in the *album iudicum* was at this period
Italian birth.   Cf. Plin. *H. N.* 33. 30 : (under Augustus) *non-
dum provinciis ad hoc munus admissis.*   Cf. Suet. *Cl.* 16.

Mommsen, *Hermes*, iv. (1870), 99.

III. THE AERARIUM AND THE FISCUS.

Reform in the administration of the Aerarium:
A. D. 44.

80.

C. I. L. vi. 1403. From the city of Rome. The original is no longer in
existence. l. 1 : *Vol(tinia) (tribu)*.

*t · do*MITIO · T · F · VOL · DECIDIO

iii VIRO · CAPITALI

*elect*O   A   TI · CLAVDIO · CAESARE
*augus*TO · GERMANICO · QVI · PRIMV*s*
5   *quaes*TOR · PER · TRIENNIVM · CITRA
*sorte*M · PRAEESSET · AERARIO · SATVRNI
PRAETORI

81.

C. I. L. vi. 916 (cf. *St. R.* ii. 558, note 3).   Preserved by the Anonymus
Einsiedlensis (see No. 34), who saw it ' in Capitolio.' The date is A. D. 46.
l. 7 : *fac*(*iendum*) *cur*(*avit*).

TI · CLAVDIVS · DRVSI · F · CAESAR · AVG
GERMANICVS   ·   PONTIF   ·   MAX
TRIB · POTEST · V · COS · III · DESIG . IIII · IMP · X · P · P
EX · S · C
5 *per* C · CALPETANVM · RANTIVM · SEDATVM · METRONIVM
M · PETRONIVM · LVRCONEM · T · SATRIVM · DECIANVM
CVRATOR*e*S · TABVLARIORVM · PVBLICORVM · FAC · CVR

The changes which had taken place in the administration of
the Aerarium from the foundation of the Principate up to
A. D. 56 are summarized by Tacitus, *Ann.* 13. 29. Claudius
though not the author of the form which it finally received,
was nevertheless responsible for the innovation which was
decisive for placing the control in the hands of the Emperor.
It is true that from the first the resources of the Aerarium
must practically have been as much at the Emperor's disposal
as those of the Fiscus (Dio Cass. 53. 16 : λόγῳ μὲν γὰρ τὰ
δημόσια ἀπὸ τῶν ἐκείνου ἀπεκέκριτο, ἔργῳ δὲ καὶ ταῦτα πρὸς τὴν
γνώμην αὐτοῦ ἀνηλίσκετο), but in dealing with its administration
Augustus did not alter the nature of the Republican system
which he found: he only attempted to improve its management by substituting for the Quaestors, first (B. C. 28) two
praefecti of praetorian rank chosen annually by the Senate
(Dio Cass. 53. 2), and afterwards (B. C. 23) two of the acting
Praetors chosen by lot (Dio Cass. 53. 32. 2).   Tacitus (l. c.)

gives as a reason for the latter change, *ambitu suffragiorum suspecto*. It had the additional merit of bringing processes between the Aerarium and private individuals, hitherto decided by the Treasury officials, within the ordinary jurisdiction of the Praetors (*St. R.* ii. 558). By the time of Claudius the working of this system had become unsatisfactory, for it was necessary in A. D. 42 to appoint a commission of three ex-Praetors to recover the arrears due to the Treasury (Dio Cass. 60. 10. 4, cf. 3), and in A. D. 44 the administration was handed over to two *quaestores aerarii* nominated by the Emperor and serving for three years (No. 80, Dio Cass. 60. 24). Finally the same reasons which had originally produced the reform of Augustus led Nero in A. D. 56 to substitute for the Quaestors, officials of higher standing and greater experience. Tac. *Ann.* 13. 29. 2 : *deerat robur aetatis eum primum magistratum capessentibus. igitur Nero praetura perfunctos et experientia probatos delegit.* The position of these *praefecti* is to be compared with that of the *praefectus annonae* (see p. 31), and marks the final stage in which the Emperor has the actual control of the Aerarium and administers it through his nominees. It is significant that on the fall of Nero the *praetores aerarii* were temporarily restored (Tac. *Hist.* 4. 9 : [A. D. 69] *nam tum a praetoribus tractabatur aerarium*).

The public records, the care of which belonged to the department of the Aerarium, had in the time of Tiberius fallen into such disorder, that a commission of three *curatores tabulariorum publicorum* (sometimes *tabularum publicarum* : *C. I. L.* x. 5182) was appointed in A.D. 16 to repair the damage and losses which had taken place (Dio Cass. 57. 16. 2). No. 81, which probably refers to some building connected with the preservation of the archives, shows that it was still in existence in A. D. 46.

The Vehiculatio transferred to the Fiscus.

82.

C. I L. iii. *Suppl.* 7251. Found at Piali, on the site of Tegea in Arcadia. In l. 7 *civitatium* appears to be a mistake for *civitates*. Notice the use of *b* for *v* in *lebare* (no doubt due to a Greek copyist or stone-cutter). It does not appear generally till the end of the second century (cf. *C. I. L.* iii. *Suppl.* p. 1309). The lower part of the inscription is illegible. The date is A. D. 49-50.

T*i* · C L A V D I V S · C A E S A R · A V G
Ger*m* A N I C V S · P O N T I F M A X
T R I B · P O T E S T · V I I I I · I M P · X V I · P · P ·
· DICIT ·
5 Cv*m* · ET · COLONIAS · ET · MVNICIPIA · NON · SOLVM
ITA*liae*E · VERVM · ETIAM · PROVINCIARVM · ITEM ·
CIVITA*ti*VM · CVIVSQVE · PROVINCIAE · LEBARE ONERIB*vs*
VEH*iculor*VM PRAEBENDORVM · SAEPE · TEM*ptavissEM*
*e*T · C*um* sat*i*S MVLTA · REMEDIA · INVENISSE · M*ihi viderer*
10 *p*OTV*it ta*MEN · NEQVITIAE HOMINVM *non satis per ea occurri*
· · · · · · · · · · · · · · · ·

The expense of providing horses and vehicles for the Imperial despatch service established by Augustus (Suet. *Aug.* 49), originally fell both in Italy and the provinces on the communities, whether Roman (l. 5 : *colonias et municipia*) or non-Roman (l. 7 : *civitates*), through which the roads passed. We gather from the fragment of this edict, that Claudius in some way remedied this state of things, probably by transferring the burden partly or wholly to the Fiscus. No other references to this reform have reached us, and there must have been a return to the old arrangement in the time of Nero (Plut. *Galba*, 8 [A.D. 69] : τῶν δ' ὑπάτων οἰκέτας δημοσίους προχειρισαμένων τὰ δόγματα κομίζοντας τῷ αὐτοκράτορι καὶ τὰ καλούμενα διπλώματα σεσημασμένα δόντων ἃ γνωρίζοντες οἱ κατὰ πόλιν ἄρχοντες ἐν ταῖς τῶν ὀχημάτων ἀμοιβαῖς ἐπιταχύνουσι τὰς προπομπὰς τῶν γραμματηφόρων). It was not until Nerva that Italy was finally relieved of the burden (Cohen, ii. p. 13, No. 143.

Eckhel, vi. 408, *vehiculatione Italiae remissa*), and the Empire generally not before Severus (*Vita Severi*, 14. 2 : *vehicularium munus a privatis ad fiscum traduxit*). The earliest evidence for the Imperial postal department (*praefectus vehiculorum, &c.*) belongs to a later period than this inscription (end of first century).

Hirschfeld, *Verwaltungsbeamten*, 190-204.

IV. THE FRONTIERS AND PROVINCES.

Recall of Germanicus: A. D. 17.   The Two Germanies.

83.

C. I. L. xiii. 7732. Altar from the north end of the bridge over the Vinxtbach. on the left bank of the Rhine between Andernach and Sinzig. Now at Brussels.

FINIBVS · ET
GENIO · LOCI
ET · I · O · M · MILIT.
LEG · XXX · V · V
5   M · MASSIÆNI
VS · SECVNDVS
ET · L · AVRELIVS
DOSSO
V · S · L · M

Finibus, et Genio loci, et I(ovi) o(ptimo) m(aximo), milit(es) leg(ionis) xxx U(lpiae) V(ictricis) M. Massiaenius Secundus et L. Aurelius Dosso v(otum) s(olverunt) l(ibentes) m(erito).

84.

C. I. L. xiii. 7731.   From the south end of the bridge.   Now at Liége.

I · O · M
ET · GENIO · LOCI
IVNONI · REGINAE
TERTINIVS
5   SEVERVS

MIL · LEG · VIII · AVG
B · F · COS · EX · VOTO
P · V · S · L · L · M

I(ovi) o(ptimo) m(aximo), et Genio loci, Iunoni Reginae, Tertinius Severus mil(es) leg(ionis) viii Aug(ustae) b(ene)f(iciarius) co(n)s(ularis) ex voto p(osuit) v(otum) s(olvens) l(ibens) l(aetus) m(erito).

These altars, erected by soldiers stationed at the boundary (*finibus* No. 83) between Upper and Lower Germany, are considerably later than the time of Tiberius (*consularis* does not appear as the title of Imperial legati of the first class before the second century), but they mark the division of the Rhine frontier between the two commands known as Upper and Lower Germany, which dates in its settled form from his reign. At first the two Germanies were not provinces proper but only a military frontier, and the justification for their existence was, partly the fact that the original province of Germany (before A.D. 9) included the German zone on the left bank of the Rhine (Caes. *B. G.* 1. 31) and had its capital there (the *ara Ubiorum*, Tac. *Ann.* 1. 57. 2), partly the necessity of creating for the consular legati of two of the most important frontier armies of the Empire, spheres of action which should be independent of the praetorian legatus of Belgica to whose province they geographically belonged. Hence all through the first century the two commanders are officially called *legatus exercitus superioris, leg. exercitus inferioris*, not *legati provinciae* (cf. the legatus in Africa, p. 130) although their spheres may be generally spoken of as *provinciae* (cf. Tac. *Ann.* 13. 53. 2: *Paulinus Pompeius et L. Vetus ea tempestate exercitui praeerant*, and notice in 4: *alienae provinciae*. Plin. *H. N.* 34. 2: [*aes*] *nuper etiam in Germania provincia repertum*. Tacitus sometimes makes use of the shortened forms, e.g. *Ann.* 3. 41. 3: *inferioris Germaniae legatus*; 4.

73 : *inferioris Germaniae pro praetore*). The division of the Rhine army into Upper and Lower had taken place before the death of Augustus, and while the government of Gaul and the command of the German legions were concentrated in one hand (Tac. *Ann.* 1. 31. 2) ; but it was not till after the recall of Germanicus in A. D. 17 that the legati attained the position which they henceforward hold.

Mommsen, *Provinces*, i. 119, note 2.

The Roman Occupation of Frisia.

85.

Votive inscription found in 1888, near Leeuwarden in Friesland, and now in the Museum there. It is the only inscription, and one of the very few Roman remains which have been discovered in this part of Holland.

Hludana, the German hearth-goddess Hlöðyn (Grimm, *Teutonic Mythology*, English translation, i. p. 256), was already known from three inscriptions of the lower Rhine (*C.I.L.* xiii. 8723, 8611, 7944). Above the inscription are the remains of a seated figure of the goddess. l. 4 : *v(otum) s(olverunt) l(ibentes) m(erito)*. Cf. *P. W.* viii. 2128.

```
        DEAE  ·  HLVDANAE
        C O N D V C T O R E S
        PISCATVS  ·  MANCIPE
        Q · VALERIO · SECV
        NDO · V · S · L · M
```

We see here one of the *societates* of *publicani* (Tac. *Ann.* 4. 6. 4) with its manager or director (Festus, p. 151 : *manceps dicitur qui quid a populo emit conducitve, quia manu sublata significat se auctorem emptionis esse*), working the fisheries in Frisia. Not only the soil of countries in which the Roman people was sovereign belonged to the Roman State, but also the rivers, lakes, and shores (for the latter cf. Celsus, *Digest.* 43. 8. 3 : *litora in quae populus Romanus imperium habet populi Romani esse arbitror*). Hence the fisheries were a regular source of revenue (Servius, *ad Georg.* 2. 161 : *Avernus et Lucrinus ... olim propter copiam piscium vectigalia magna praestabant*, cf. Polyb. 6. 17. 2). At the date of this inscription therefore the Frisii must have been regarded as subjects, which was hardly the case during the first period of their connection with Rome (after B.C. 12 when Drusus τοὺς Φρει-σίους ᾠκειώσατο, Dio Cass. 54. 32. 2) when their position was probably analogous to that of the Batavi (Tac. *Hist.* 5. 25. 4), though they were less independent as being governed by a *praefectus* and paying a tribute of hides *in usus militares* (Tac. *Ann.* 4. 72. 2). After their revolt in A. D. 28 (Tac. l. c.) they were independent till A D. 47 when they submitted to Corbulo and were apparently reduced to the condition of subjects (Tac. *Ann.* 11. 19. 2 : *idem senatum, magistratus, leges imposuit, ac ne iussa exuerent praesidium immunivit*). It is true that almost immediately after, Claudius ordered the withdrawal of all the garrisons from the right bank of the Rhine (Tac. *Ann.* 11. 19. 7), but Frisia must have remained Roman territory, for we find soldiers for the Roman army levied there down to a comparatively late period (*C. I. L.* iii. p. 866 *cohors I Frisiavonum* in Diploma of A.D. 105, p. 873 of A. D. 124. *Notitia Dignitatum*, 40. 36). It is possible that the part of Friesland in which this inscription was found may have been regarded as within the delta of the Rhine (Plin. *H. N.* 4. 101 : *in Rheno ipso . . . nobilissima Batavorum insula et Cannenefatum, et aliae Frisiorum . . . quae sternuntur inter Helium ac Flevum*), but Tacitus calls them a *transrhenanus populus* (*Ann.* 4. 72, cf. *Germ.* 34 : [*Frisii*] *usque ad Oceanum Rheno praetexuntur*), and this was probably one of the cases where the military did not coincide with the actual frontier of the Empire (cf. Mommsen, *Prov.* i. 126).

C. Zangemeister, *Korrespondenzblatt der Westdeutschen Zeitschrift*, 1889. Jan. col. 2.

P. U. Boissevain, *Mnemosyne*, xvi. (1888), 439.

The Conquest of Britain.

86.

C. I. L. vi. 920. Inscriptions from a triumphal arch of Claudius at Rome, erected in A.D. 51-52. The fragments were found near the line of the Via Flaminia, together with a series of inscriptions in honour of members of the Imperial family (*C. I. L.* vi. 921 = *D.* 222). Germanicus, Antonia Augusta, the Empress Agrippina, Nero, Octavia). Probably therefore the arch was of the same type as that of Ticinum (No. 34), and crowned by statues of Claudius and his immediate relations.

> TI · CLAV*dio drusi f. cai*SARI
> AVG V*sto germani*CO
> PONTIFIC*i maximo trib. potes*TAT · XĪ
> COS · V̄ · IM*p. xxi*(?), *patri pa*TRIAI
> 5   SENATVS · P*opulusque* · RO*manus q*VOD
> REGES · BRIT*anniai* XI *devictos sine*
> VLLA · IACTVR*a in deditionem acceperit*
> GENTESQVE · B*arbaras trans oceanum*
> PRĪMVS · IN DICI*onem populi romani redegerit*

87.

B. M. C. Emp. i, Claud. 32. Eckhel, vi. 240. Aureus of A. D. 46.

Obv. TI. CLAVD. CAESAR AVG. P. M. TR. P. VI IMP. XI. Head of Claudius.

Rev. Triumphal arch on which is inscribed : DE BRITANN(*is*).

This inscription belongs to the triumphal arch erected at Rome to commemorate the expedition of Claudius to Britain in A. D. 43. Dio Cass. 60. 22 : ἁψῖδας τροπαιοφόρους, τὴν μὲν ἐν τῇ πόλει τὴν δὲ ἐν τῇ Γαλατίᾳ, ὅθεν ἐς τὴν Βρεττανίαν ἐξαναχθεὶς ἐπεραιώθη, γένεσθαι ἐψηφίσαντο. The coin No. 87, which illustrates the same event, represents an arch of a different type, and is some years earlier than the structure to which No. 86 belonged which was not completed before A. D. 51. By that time Caratacus has been made a prisoner. His brothers *in deditionem accepti* (Tac. *Ann.* 12. 35. 7) are no doubt included among the *XI reges*. The conjectural restoration *trans Oceanum* in l. 8 is made probable by the emphasis which was laid at the time on this aspect of the expedition (Suet. *Cl.* 17 : *navalem coronam fastigio Palatinae domus iuxta civicam fixit, traiecti et quasi domiti Oceani insigne*).

The conquest of Britain was the first important departure from the policy laid down by Augustus *coercendi intra terminos imperii* (Tac. *Ann.* 1. 11. 7), a policy largely dictated by financial considerations (cf. Strabo, 2. 5. 8, p. 115, 4. 5. 3, p. 200 : τουλάχιστον μὲν γὰρ ἑνὸς τάγματος χρῄζοι ἂν καὶ ἱππικοῦ τινος). As such it proportionately impressed the Empire at large, and we have an indication of the interest aroused by the event in the fact that about the same time an arch (probably a copy of the one at Rome) was erected at Cyzicus in honour of Claudius as *devi[ctori regum XI] Britanniae. C. I. L.* iii. *Suppl.* 7061, vi. p. 841.

Mommsen, *Provinces*, ch. v. and esp. *The Roman Occupation of Britain*, by F. Haverfield and G. Macdonald (Oxford, 1924), pp. 100 ff.

Roads in Dalmatia.

88.

C. I. L. iii. 3198. *Suppl.* 10156. On two fragments built into the cathedral at Spalato. The date is A.D. 16–17.

(*a*)   *ti. c*AESAR · DĪVI · AVGVSTi · F
    *aug*VSTVS · IMP · PONT · MAX ·
    trib. POTEST · XĪĪX · COS · ĪI ·

    viam A   COLONIA   SALONITAN*a*
    *m*VNIT VICI

(*b*)   *et idem viam?*
    *mu*NIT AD *sum*MVM MONTEM DĪTIONVM
    VLCIRVM   PER MILLIA PASSVVM
        A · SALONIS LXXVIID   *sic*
    P · DOLABELLA LEG PRO
        PR

89.

C. I. L. iii. 3201. *Suppl.* 10159. In the same place as the last. The date is
A. D. 19-20. In l. 4 the beginning of ιne name of the *castellum* may be *Lip.* or
Lib. In ll. 7, 8, the highly probable suggestions of Bulić mentioned in *C. I. L.*
iii. *Suppl.* have been adopted.

```
ti.cAESAR   ·   DIVI   ·   AVGVSTI   ·   F
auGVSTVS   ·   IMP   ·   PONTIF   ·   MAX
TRIB   ·   POTEST   ·   XXI   ·   cOS   III
VIAM · A · SALONIS AD HE(?) cASTEL
5   DAESITIATIVM   PER   Mil.   passVVM
CLVI · MVNIT
ET · IDEM · VIAM AD BAsante(?) fluMEN
QVOD DIVIDIT BIStuates a DitionIBVS
A · SALONIS · MVNit per millia passVVM
10   CLVIII
```

On the suppression of the general rising in Illyricum (A. D.
6–9) the province was divided, and the southern portion or
Dalmatia, the official title of which before the Flavian period
seems to have been Illyricum Superius (compare *C. I. L.* iii.
1741 = *D.* 938 in honour of Dolabella, the *legatus* of No. 88, by
the *civitates superioris provinciae Hillyrici*, with 4013, under
Domitian, the earliest instance in an inscription of *legatus pro
praetore provinciae Delmatiae*), although not a frontier province, received, like Hispania Citerior and for the same
reason, a garrison of two legions (Tac. *Ann.* 4. 5. 5) numbered VII and XI. For the natural difficulties which stood
in the way of the spread of Roman civilisation in the interior,
see Mommsen, *Provinces*, i. 203. Nevertheless the submission
of the country was so far secured, that before A. D. 66 the
garrison was reduced to one legion (Josephus, *B. J.* 2. 16. 4:
Δαλμάται . . . νῦν οὐχ ὑφ᾽ ἑνὶ τάγματι ῾Ρωμαίων ἡσυχίαν ἄγουσιν;
The Seventh Legion was sent to Moesia), and under Vespasian dispensed with altogether. To this end the action of
Tiberius in carrying the roads, to which Nos. 88 and 89 refer,
into the uncivilised eastern districts must have contributed

(compare his similar activity in the North-West of Spain).   It will be noticed that the latter are still in the tribal stage of organisation, with *castella* as centres of the *gentes* or *civitates* (No. 89. 4).   The localities mentioned cannot be identified with certainty, but it is clear from the distances that the roads penetrated to the regions bordering on Moesia, important for their mines.

Archaeologia, 49. (1885), A. J. Evans, *Antiquarian Researches in Illyricum*, esp. pp. 1–14.

Moesia under Tiberius.

90.

C. I. L. v. 1838.   On a bronze tablet found at Zuglio (Iulium Carnicum), and now in the Museum at Cividale.   Apparently C. Baebius Atticus became a magistrate in his native town (Iulium Carnicum belonged to the Claudian tribe), and a statue was erected to him there (cf. analogous case, No. 100) by one of the communities subject to him as Procurator of Noricum.   After passing from the post of highest centurion to the equestrian service he receives a second time the rank of *primus pilus* on the conclusion of the first part of that career (the *militiae equestres*) in order that before proceeding to the higher part (the *procuratelae*, &c.) he may obtain the advantages (esp. pecuniary) which belonged to the first centurion on his discharge (Mommsen on *C. I. L.* v. 867; and cf. H. Karbe, *Dissert Halenses*, iv. 418).   For the *praemia* cf. Suet. *Cal.* 44 : *plerisque centurionum ... primos pilos ademit ... commoda emeritae militiae ad sescentorum milium summam recidit.*

C · BAEBIO · P · F · CLA

ATTICO

$\overline{\text{II}}$ VIR · I · *d* · PRIMOPIL

LEG · $\overline{\text{V}}$ · MACEDONIC · PRAEF

5   C*i*VITATIVM · MOESIAE · ET

TREBALLIA*e* · *pra*EF · *ci*VITAT

IN · ALPIB · MARITVMIS · T*r* · MIL · COH

$\overline{\text{VIII}}$ · PR · PRIMOPIL · ITER · PROCVRATOR

TI · CLAVDI · CAESARIS · AVG · GERMANICI

10   IN NORICO

CIVITAS

SAEVATVM · ET · LAIANCORVM

C. Baebio P. f. Cla(udia) (tribu) Attico, II vir(o) i(ure)

[d(icundo)], primopil(o) leg(ionis) V Macedonic(ae), praef(ecto)
c[i]vitatium Moesiae et Treballia[e], [pra]ef(ecto) [ci]vitat(ium)
in Alpib(us) Maritumis, t[r(ibuno)] mil(itum) coh(ortis) VIII
pr(aetoriae), primopil(o) iter(um), procurator(i) Ti. Claudi
Caesaris Aug(usti) Germanici in Norico, civitas Servatum et
Laiancorum.

91.

C. I. L. iii. 1698. One of three similar inscriptions cut in the rock by the side
of the Roman road near Boljetin in Serbia on the south bank of the Danube,
close to the Iron Gates. The date is A.D. 33–34.

TI · CAESARE · AVG F
AVGVSTO · IMPERATOR
PONT MAX · TR · POT · X̄X̄X̄V
LEG · ĪĪĪĪ · SCYT · LEG · V̄ MACED

Before the time of Claudius the frontier of the lower
Danube was divided between the province of Moesia and
the kingdom of Thrace. For the latter, see No. 92. Moesia
was conquered as early as B.C. 29 (Dio Cass. 51. 23–27).
The first mention of a legatus is in A.D. 6, Dio Cass. 55. 29.
3; but No. 90 is an indication that in the time of Tiberius
(under whom the *praefectura* of ll. 4–6 would probably come)
the organisation of the province was still in the rudimentary
stage and that it was necessary for special reasons to place
these native communities within the province under a *praefectus*. Cf. p. 39, for similar cases, to which may be added
C. I. L. ix. 2564: ... *Marcelli (centurionis) leg. XI Cl[aud.
pr]aef. civitatis Maeze[iorum]*. 5363: *L. Volcacio Primo
praef. Coh. I Noricor. in Pann(onia), praef. ripae Danuui et
civitatium duar(um) Boior(um) et Azalior(um)*. No. 91 relates
to the construction of the military road which connected the
stations along the right bank of the Danube. The headquarters of the two legions (IV Scythica, V Macedonica, l. 4)
which then formed the garrison of the province are unknown.

Mommsen, *Provinces*, i. 213 and note.

The Province of Thrace under Claudius and Nero.

92.

C. I. L. iii. 6123.   Found in a village at the foot of the southern slope of the Haemus, north of Philippopolis. The date is A. D. 61. In the first line the name of Nero seems to have been erased after his death.

nero   claudius

DIVI · CLAVDI · F

GERM · CAESARIS · N ·

TI · CAESARIS · AVG ·

5   PRON · DIVI · AVG · ABN

CAESAR · AVG · GERM

PONTIF · MAX · TRIB · POT

V̄ĪĪĪ · IMP · V̄ĪĪĪ · COS · IIII

P · P

10   TABERNAS · ET · PRAETORIA

PER · VIAS · MILITARES

FIERI · IVSSIT · PER

TI · *i*VLIVM · *i*VSTVM · PROC

PROVINCIAE · THRAC

The task of defending the lower Danube frontier was originally divided between the governor of the province of Moesia for the western part, and the vassal princes of Thrace for the eastern (cf. Tac. *Ann.* 2. 65. 5: [*Rhescuporis*] *bellum adversus Bastarnas Scythasque praetendens novis peditum et equitum copiis sese firmabat*). After Claudius, on the occasion of the murder of the last king Rhoemetalces in A. D. 46, had completed the process of annexation begun by Tiberius in A. D. 19 (Tac. *Ann.* 2. 67. 4), Thrace was constituted as a province of the second class under a Procurator (l. 13). Apparently soon after, a system of military roads was laid out (l. 11), mainly no doubt with a view to the consolidation of Roman rule among a people which had made desperate efforts for independence (Tac. *Ann.* 3. 38. 4 sqq., 4. 46, Syn-

cellus, p. 631, *ed. Bonn* : Κλαύδιος ... Κέλτους καὶ Βρεταννοὺς
ὅπλοις ἀνδρείως ὑπηγάγετο, ὁμοίως καὶ Θρᾷκας, ἀναιρεθέντος αὐτῶν
τοῦ βασιλέως Ῥυμητάλκου ὑπὸ τῆς ἰδίας γαμετῆς. The latter war
is no doubt referred to by Tacitus, *Ann.* 12. 63. 3, where he
speaks of the people of Byzantium in A. D. 53 as *Thraecio
... bello recens fessos. C.I.L.* ii. 3272, quoted on p. 119, belongs
to this time). No. 92 relates to the completion of this work
under Nero by the erection of resting-places for ordinary
soldiers, &c. (*tabernae*) as well as for State officials (*praetoria*),
and points generally to a more settled state of things. Certainly shortly after this date a comparatively small force was
sufficient to preserve order in the country. (Josephus, *B. J.*
2. 16. 4: [speech of Agrippa in A.D. 66] τί δὲ Θρᾷκες ; . . . .
οὐχὶ δισχιλίοις Ῥωμαίων ὑπακούουσι φρουροῖς ;) It must be
remembered however that the legions of Moesia were close
at hand. For the relation of Thrace to the superior province
cf. Tac. *Hist.* 1. 11. 3: *Thraecia et quae aliae procuratoribus
cohibentur, ut cuique exercitui vicinae, ita in favorem aut odium
contactu valentiorum agebantur.*

Mommsen, *Provinces*, i. 209 sqq. esp. 212.
Mommsen in *Ephemeris Epigraphica*, ii. 256-258.

Roman Rule beyond the Danube under Nero.

93.

C. I. L. xiv. 3608. On the mausoleum of the Plautii which stands by the side
of the Via Tiburtina near the bridge over the Anio. Various grammatical errors
in the original have been corrected in the text here given.

Ti. Plautio M. f. Ani(ensi) (tribu)
    Silvano Aeliano,
      pontif(ici), sodali Aug(ustali),
III vir(o) a(uro) a(rgento) a(ere) f(lando) f(eriundo), q(uaestori)
      Ti. Caesaris,
5   legat(o) leg(ionis) V in Germania,
      pr(aetori) urb(ano), legat(o) et comiti Claud(ii)

Caesaris in Brittannia, consuli,
procos. Asiae, legat(o) pro praet(ore) Moesiae,
In qua plura quam centum mill(ia)
10   ex numero Transdanuvianor(um)
ad praestanda tributa cum coniugib(us)
ac liberis et principibus aut regibus suis
transduxit. Motum orientem Sarmatar(um)
compressit, quamvis partem magnam exercitus
15   ad expeditionem in Armeniam misisset.
Ignotos ante aut infensos p(opulo) R(omano) reges signa
Romana adoraturos in ripam quam tuebatur
perduxit. Regibus Bastarnarum et
Rhoxolanorum filios, Dacorum fratres
20   captos aut hostibus ereptos remisit ; ab
aliquis eorum opsides accepit ; per quae pacem
provinciae et confirmavit et protulit ;
Scytharum quoque rege a Cherronensi,
quae est ultra Borustenen, opsidione summoto.
25 Primus ex ea provincia magno tritici modo
annonam p(opuli) R(omani) adlevavit.   Hunc legatum in
Hispaniam ad praefectur(am) urbis remissum
senatus in praefectura triumphalibus
ornamentis honoravit, auctore imp.
30   Caesare Augusto Vespasiano, verbis ex
oratione eius q(uae) i(nfra) s(cripta) s(unt) :
Moesiae ita praefuit, ut non debuerit in
me differri honor triumphalium eius
ornamentorum ; nisi quod latior ei
35   contigit mora titulus praefecto urbis.
Hunc in eadem praefectura urbis imp. Caesar
Aug. Vespasianus iterum co(n)s(ulem) fecit.

The principal fact which we learn from the somewhat confused statements of this inscription, is the extension of Roman
rule over the northern shores of the Black Sea which took

place under Nero. The various operations recorded are given
in geographical (and therefore not necessarily chronological)
order from West to East, the Sarmatae (l. 13) affecting rather
the middle Danube (cf. the locality of the Suebo-Sarmatian
war of Domitian in which the Iazyges in the region of the
Theiss took part; Dio Cass. 67. 5. 2), while the Bastarnae
and Rhoxolani (l. 18) belong to the district north-west of the
Black Sea. The last part of the narrative (l. 23) refers to
the Tauric Chersonnese, where the free Greek city Heraclea
Chersonesus (Sebastopol) had it seems been besieged by the
Scythians. The Roman interference here referred to must
have resulted in a Roman occupation, for in A. D. 66 the
Crimea and the neighbouring parts were regarded as a subject
country and held by a Roman garrison (speech of Agrippa
in Josephus, *B. J.* 2. 16. 4: τί δεῖ λέγειν ... τὸ τῶν Ταύρων
φῦλον, Βοσπορανούς τε καὶ περίοικα τοῦ Πόντου καὶ τῆς Μαιώτιδος
ἔθνη νῦν δὲ τρισχιλίοις ὁπλίταις ὑποτάσσεται, καὶ τεσσαράκοντα
νῆες μακραὶ τὴν πρὶν ἄπλωτον καὶ ἀγρίαν εἰρηνεύουσι θάλασσαν).
It was in A. D. 63 that Nero deposed Cotys and annexed the
client kingdom of the Bosporus (in that year its coins become
purely Imperial and omit all reference to the native rulers;
Sallet, *Zeitschrift f. Numismatik*, iv. (1877), 304), and this
probably settles the date of the expedition of Plautius Silvanus, for, as has been shown by Domaszewski (l. c. infr.),
the statement about the reduction of the army of Moesia in
l. 14 refers to the transference of the Fifth Legion to the East
about A. D. 62 (Tac. *Ann.* 15. 6. 5: *quae recens e Moesis excita
erat*) whither it had been preceded by the other legion of
Moesia in A. D. 57 (Tac. *Ann.* 13. 7), so that the repulse of
the Sarmatians cannot have taken place before that year and
was carried out, together with the occupation of the Crimea,
by means of the Eighth Legion which had been moved to
Moesia at the time of the conquest of Thrace in A. D. 46, and
remained there till the end of Nero's reign (*C. I. L.* ii. 3272 =
W. 1626 *a*: [*Q. Cor*]*nelio Valeriano* ... *praef*(*ecto*) *vexillari-*

orum in Trachia XV [*a leg(ione) IIII Scythica* (?) *a leg(ione) V Mace*]*donica a leg(ione) VIII Augusta &c. statuis coroni*[*s donato, &c.*]. Mommsen, *Eph. Epigr.* ii. 259, note 2. Domaszewski, l. c. infr. p. 211. Hence the objection that in A. D. 62 not a part but the whole of the Moesian army had been sent away falls to the ground. Cf. *W.* i. p. 369, H. Dessau on *C. I. L.* xiv. 3608). The fact that the Roman era of the city of Tyra began in A. D. 57 (*C. I. L.* iii. 781, l. 44. Bruns, *Fontes*, p. 263) must have some relation to these events, and may show that the submission of the Bastarnae (ll. 18–22) took place at that time, and the advance beyond the Borysthenes about five years later. Plautius probably became Proconsul of Asia (l. 8) in succession to Iunius Silanus who died during his tenure of that province in A. D. 54 (Tac. *Ann.* 13. 1), and would in that case have entered on his command in Moesia in A. D. 55.

H. Dessau in *C. I. L.* xiv. 394.

A. v. Domaszewski, *Die Dislocation des römischen Heeres in Jahre 66 n. Chr., Rheinisches Museum*, xlvii. (1892), 208–213.

Growth of Towns beside the Frontier Camps. The Canabae.

94.

C. I. L. v. 5747. In the Church of S. Maurizio at Monza. l. 2 : *Ouf*(*entina*) (*tribu*).

```
     C · SERTORIVS · L · F
    OVF · TE . . . . . VS
   VETERANVS · LEG : XVI
   CVRATOR · CIVIVM · ROMANor
        MOGONTIACI
```

This inscription, which cannot be much later than the time of Nero when the Sixteenth Legion was transferred to Lower Germany (Tac. *Hist.* 1. 55. 2, cf. *Ann.* 1. 37. 4), is one of the earliest pieces of evidence we possess about the organisation

of the settlements which grew up beside the fixed quarters
of the legions especially on the Rhine and Danube frontiers.
The *cives Romani* here mentioned are *negotiatores* and others,
attracted to the camp at Mainz, partly to supply the wants
of a large stationary body of soldiers, partly in order to traffic
under their protection with the neighbouring provincials or
barbarians. The importance sometimes attained by these
settlements is shown by the description given by Tacitus of
that at Vetera in A. D. 69 (*Hist.* 4. 22): *longae pacis opera
haud procul castris in modum municipii exstructa.* Such
communities would as time went on require an independent
organisation. It will be noticed that the quasi-magistrate of
No. 94 (cf. *summus curator c(ivium) R(omanorum) provinc(iac)
Lug(dunensis), W.* 2224) is a veteran ; and in the case of
most of these settlements, veterans, not provided for elsewhere
by a *deductio,* form an important element. As early as the
time of Augustus or Tiberius we hear of communities of
veterans under a *curator* (*C. I. L.* v. 5832 : *P. Tutilius P. f.
O[uf.] veteranus . . . curator vete[ran(orum)].* He died A. D.
29), and hence it is natural to find these composite communities outside the Legionary camps organised under a similar
official. Owing to their origin as centres of trade, these
places became known as *canabae,* from the popular name of
a shed or warehouse of more or less temporary character (cf.
W. 2230, 2506, inscriptions of *curatores corporis negotiatorum
vinariorum Luguduni in kanabis consistentium.* 'Canova,' the
representative of *canaba* in Italian, is used for a wine-cellar.
See De Vit's *Forcellini,* for other illustrations, and cf. in the
inscription referred to p. 31, *C. I. L.* vi. 1585: *impensa de
casulis item cannabis et aedificiis idoneis*). The organisation
of the Canabae, which were called not by any local name but
by that of the legion with which they were connected, consisted of the *curator* (whose full title would be *curator veteranorum et civium Romanorum qui consistunt ad canabas legionis*), subordinate officials (*quaestor* and *actor*: for Mainz,

cf. *D.* 7077, 2469), and an *ordo* of *decuriones* (for Mainz cf. *D.* 7078, 7079). The *curator* was apparently elected (*C.I.L.* iii. 2733= *W.* 1492 from Aequum in Dalmatia : *Sex. Iu[lius] ... Silvanus, summus c[urator c(ivium) R(omanorum)] suffragio [veteranor(um) ?] leg(ionis) VII, &c.*).

The community at Mainz was singularly late in receiving municipal rights (not before Diocletian). Most of the Canabae were converted into *municipia* or *coloniae* before the third century, in the earlier cases on the occasion of the moving of the legion, but from the time of Trajan onwards the new town often existed by the side of the military quarters (e. g. Carnuntum, which became a *municipium* under Hadrian, was the station of the Fourteenth Legion from the second to the fourth century, *C. I. L.* iii. 550). The transition from the Canabae to the full municipal organisation was formed by a constitution of a purely civil type analogous to that of the pagus or vicus, under *magistri* (e. g. *C. I. L.* iii. 6166).

Mommsen, *Hermes*, vii. (1873), 299.

E Kornemann, *De civibus Romanis in provinciis imperii consistentibus*. Berlin, 1892, 80 sqq.

Tiberius and the Cities of Asia.

95.

C.I.L. x. 1624. Pedestal which probably supported a colossal statue of Tiberius. On its sides are allegorical figures in bas-relief representing the fourteen cities of Asia with the names beneath. The dedication to Tiberius occupies the middle of the principal face. Found at Puteoli and now in the Museum at Naples. The date is A. D. 30. The names which accompany that of Sardes seem to have been added later, and no doubt refer to the personifications represented with the figure of the city on the sculpture. Professor Ramsay has pointed out to me that the first of these is probably Εὐθηνία, who appears in other municipal cults in Asia (see *Journal of Philology*, xi. (1882), 144).

PHILADELPHEA   TMOLVS   CYME

TEMNOS   CIBYRA   MYRINA   EPHESOS   APOLLONIDEA   HYRCA*nia*

magnesia

TI · CAESARI · DIVI
AVGVSTI · F · DIVI
IVLI · N · AVGVSTO
PONTIF · MAXIMO · COS · IIII
5   IMP · VIII · TRIB · POTESTAT · XXXII
AVGVSTALES
RES · PVBLICA
RESTITVIT

*eu*tHENIA · SAR*des* · VLLORON

MOSTENE   *aeg*AE   *hieroc*AESAREA

96.

B. M. C. Emp. i, Tib. 70.   Eckhel, vi. 192.   Sestertius of A.D. 22.

Obverse.   TI. CAESAR DIVI AVG. F. AVGVST. P. M. TR. POT.
XXIIII round S. C.

Reverse.   CIVITATIBVS ASIAE RESTITVTIS.   Seated figure of
Tiberius.

The earthquake of A. D. 17 which ruined twelve cities of
Asia (Tac. *Ann.* 2. 47.   Plin. *H. N.* 2. 200: *maximus terrae
memoria mortalium motus*), was followed by another in A. D.
23 which affected only Cibyra (Tac. *Ann.* 4. 13).   In both
cases Tiberius granted remissions of taxation, and in the
first he further provided funds for the restoration.   Ephesus
must have suffered and been relieved in the same way about
A. D. 29 or 30 (i.e. it is not mentioned in Tacitus who is
complete up to A. D. 29, *Ann.* 5. 5, but its name occurs on
this monument of A. D. 30).   In A. D. 22 a monument was
erected at Rome by the restored cities of Asia in gratitude
to Tiberius (No. 96), which is thus described by Phlegon
Trallianus (*Fr.* 42 in Müller, *Frag. Hist. Graec.* iii): ἀνθ' ὧν
κολοσσόν τε αὐτῷ κατασκευάσαντες ἀνέθεσαν παρὰ τῷ τῆς 'Αφρο-
δίτης ἱερῷ ὅ ἐστιν ἐν τῇ 'Ρωμαίων ἀγορᾷ καὶ τῶν πόλεων ἑκάστης
ἐφεξῆς ἀνδριάντας παρέστησαν (*C. I. G.* 3450 from Sardis is
perhaps part of the decree of the towns relating to its erection.
Cibyra is included).   It was no doubt after this model that
the Augustales of Puteoli erected the monument to which
No. 95 belongs, and apparently on the occasion of the Emperor's liberality to Ephesus.   Their action is explained by
the fact that Puteoli was, in the last centuries of the Republic
and the first of the Empire, the great Italian port for the
trade of the Mediterranean (Statius, *Silv.* 3. 5. 75: *litora
mundi hospita*) and especially of its eastern half.   For special
references to a connection between Puteoli and the province

of Asia, cf. *C.I.L.* x. 1797, dedication to L. Calpurnius Capitolinus (cf. No. 44) by the *mercatores qui Alexandr(iai) Asiai Syriai negotiantur,* and the epitaphs there of persons who had come from the West of Asia Minor, collected in Beloch, *Campanien,* pp. 121, 122 (e.g. 178=Kaibel, *Inscr. Graec. Sic. et Ital.* 847: Κόιντος Καλπούρνιος Ῥοῦφος Ἐφέσιος). The Augustales therefore, as representing the class of *negotiatores,* were commercially, and in some cases perhaps patriotically, interested in the welfare of the cities of Asia; while their connection with the worship of the Emperor was an additional motive for the honour paid to Tiberius. For the divine attributes of the statue as represented on the coins, see Eckhel, vi. 193.

Puteoli had attained a position of great commercial importance before the destruction of Delos by Mithridates (Strabo, 10. 5. 4, p. 486), but its supremacy was assured by that event (cf. Festus, p. 122: *minorem Delum Puteolos esse dixerunt quod Delos aliquando maximum emporium fuerit totius orbis terrarum cui successit postea Puteolanum . . . unde Lucilius: Inde Dicaearcheum populos Delumque minorem.* Delos never recovered. Strabo, l. c.: διετέλεσε μέχρι νῦν ἐνδεῶς πράττουσα). It is however to the first period of the Empire that its greatest prosperity belongs. The construction of the great harbour works at the mouth of the Tiber by Claudius and Trajan, sealed its fate by depriving the port of the chief reason for its existence.

> *C. I. L.* x. 182, 183.
> Beloch, *Campanien,* p. 114 sqq.

Occupation of Armenia: A. D. 64.

97.

C. I. L. iii. *Suppl.* 6741. One of three similar inscriptions found near Charput in Armenia. Nero commonly appears in inscriptions without the *praenomen imperatoris,* but the use of Imperator after the cognomina in addition to the

numbered *acclamatio imperatoria* is quite irregular.   *Fecit* is to be supplied with
the whole sentence.   The date is A. D. 64.

NERO · CLAVDIᴠs

CAESAR · AVG GERM̃Nᴄᴠs

IMP · PONT · MX TRIB · POT · X̄Ī

COS Īīīī · IMP · V̄Īīīī · PAT P

5   CN   DOMITIO   ᴄRBVLONE

LEG · AVG · PRO · PR

T AVRELIO · FVLVᵒ LEᴳ N̄ᴳ

LEG · Īīī · GAL ·

This inscription belongs to the period of the second occupation of Armenia by the army of Corbulo (A.D. 63–66), when
by an overwhelming display of force (Tac. *Ann.* 15. 25, 26)
the Roman government had extracted from Vologasus the
all-important concession that Tiridates, the Parthian nominee
for the throne of Armenia, should go to Rome and receive
his investiture at the hands of the Emperor (Tac. *Ann.* 15.
29).   The exceptional command created for Corbulo during
the Armenian war, consisted in the first instance of the (previously procuratorial, Tac. *Ann.* 12. 49) province of Cappa-
docia with the title *legatus Augusti pro praetore*, and half of
the army of Syria (the III Gallica of No. 97 and the VI
Ferrata), to which Galatia seems to have been added (Tac.
Ann. 13. 35. 4).   In the second stage of the war (A. D. 63)
not only was the number of his forces increased (Tac. *Ann.*
15. 26. which shows that the Third Legion was again employed), but he received what was practically an *imperium
maius* in the neighbouring (praetorian) provinces and inferior
administrative districts (Tac. *Ann.* 15. 25. 6 : *scribitur tetrar-
chis ac regibus praefectisque et procuratoribus et qui praetorum
finitimas provincias regebant, iussis Corbulonis obsequi*).   It
will be noticed that these extended powers are not specially
recognised in his official title on the inscription.

These inscriptions must have been connected with some

permanent Roman work, no doubt the fortress, which from another name of Charput, Hisn Ziâd, has been identified with the *Ziata castellum* mentioned by Ammianus Marcellinus (19. 6, A.D. 359). As Charput is on the eastern side of the Euphrates, it was probably erected rather for purposes of military occupation than of frontier defence. Still Sophene, in which it is situated, was a principality distinct from Armenia (Tac. *Ann.* 13. 7. 2), and under Roman protection.

> Mommsen, *Hermes*, xv. (1880), 294.
> Furneaux, *Tacitus*, ii. p. 125, note 6.

Military Frontier of Africa : A. D. 14.

98.

C. I. L. viii. 10023. Milestone found between Tacapae on the Syrtis Minor and Capsa. The praenomen of Asprenas (Lucius) has been omitted by mistake : it occurs in another example from the same road (*C. I. L.* viii. 10018). *Tacapes* appears to be a mistake for *Tacapas*, *Tacapae* being the common form of the name. It is irregular in inscriptions of this class for the names of both Emperor and Governor to appear in the nominative ; and the name of the legion which performed the work is generally either preceded by *per* or followed by *fecit*. The date is A.D. 14

```
        IMP · CAES · AVGVS
        TI · F · AVGVSTVS TRI
        P O T              X̄V̄I
        ASPRENAS  COS  PR
   5    COS  VII  VIR  EPVLo
        NVM  VIAM  EX  CAST
        HIBERNIS  TACAPES
        MVNIENDAM  CVRAVIT
        LEG · ĪĪĪ . AVG ·
            C I . . . . .
```

The road to which this milestone belonged must have been finished by Asprenas (Tac. *Ann.* 1. 53. 9) in the first days of the reign of Tiberius. Augustus died on Aug. 19th (Suet. *Aug.*

100), and his consecration took place on Sept. 17th (*C. I. L.* i. ·p. 324 : *Fasti Amiternini*, for that day : *Fer(iae) ex s. c. q(uod) e(o) d(ie) divo Augusto honores caelestes a senatu decreti*), but as he is not here called *divus*, the inscription must have been put up between the two dates, or rather, before Asprenas had received information of the latter event. The inscription assumes that Tiberius would retain the (hereditary) *praenomen imperatoris*, which as a matter of fact he renounced (Suet. *Tib.* 26), and which is very rarely found in his inscriptions.

The real importance however of this inscription is due to the light which it throws on military arrangements in Africa under Augustus and his immediate successors. It shows that before A. D. 14 the headquarters of the African legion had been already fixed at the foot of the northern slope of the Mons Aurasius where they remained for more than two centuries. Only two milestones of the road which connected them with the eastern coast have been discovered, but the numbers on these, though mutilated (in 10018 found at Tacapae the number was under CC but over CLX), make it clear that the starting-point of the road, and therefore the headquarters themselves, were at Theveste, which is in round numbers 200 miles distant from Tacapae, and moreover the general centre of the road-system of this part of Africa in the first century (*C. I. L.* viii. p. 859). An additional piece of evidence in favour of Theveste is the similar road made by the legion under Trajan to connect it with the north coast at Hippo Regius (*C. I. L.* viii. 10037). It was therefore a relatively small change when Hadrian moved the headquarters from the eastern end of the Aurasius range to the western at Lambaesis. But it must be remembered that by that time the Roman frontier ran along the southern base of the range, whereas under Tiberius the legion at Theveste must have confronted the mountains as the stronghold of Tacfarinas and the Musulamii who are described as living ὑπὸ τὸ Αὖδον ὄρος

(Ptol. 4. 3. 24) and apparently on the side which faced the Sahara (Tac. *Ann.* 2. 52. 3 : *solitudinibus Africae propinqua*).

C. I. L. viii. xxi, 859, 860.
Cagnat, *L'Armée Romaine d'Afrique*, 497 sqq.

The Command of the African Legion taken from the Proconsul.

99.

C. I. L. viii. *Suppl.* 14603. Epitaph from the site of Simitthus (Africa Proconsularis). For *hostem* in l. 7 cf. *C. I. L.* viii. 4333 : *in civitatem sua.* 9381 : *ex Germania superiorem.*

```
        L · FLAMINIVS · D · F · ARN
           MIL · LEG · III · AVG
        7 · IVLI · LONGI · DILECTO
        LECTVS · AB · M · SILANO · MIL
 5      ANNIS · XIX · IN · PRAESIDIO
        VT · ESSET · IN · SALTO · PHILOMV
        SIANO · AB · HOSTEM · IN · PVGN
        OCCISSVS · VIXIT · PIE
             A N N I S  XL
10             H · S · E
```

L. Flaminius D(ecimi) f. Arn(ensi) (tribu), mil(es) leg(ionis) III Aug(ustae) (centuria) Iuli Longi, dilecto lectus ab M. Silano, mil(itavit) annis XIX in praesidio ut esset in Salto Philomusiano, ab hostem in pugna occissus. Vixit pie annis XL. H(ic) s(itus) e(st).

This inscription illustrates the state of things with regard to the military command in Africa after the change made by Gaius. That change is described by Tacitus (*Hist.* 4. 48) : *legio in Africa auxiliaque tutandis imperii finibus sub divo Augusto Tiberioque principibus proconsuli parebant. mox C. Caesar turbidus animi et Marcum Silanum obtinentem Africam* (A.D. 32–38) *metuens, ablatam proconsuli legionem misso in eam rem legato tradidit. aequatus inter duos beneficiorum numerus, et mixtis utriusque mandatis discordia quaesita auctaque pravo certamine.* L. Flaminius (probably a native of Carthage, which belonged to the tribus Arnensis : *Eph. Epigr.* iv. 537) entered the Third Legion while the Proconsul still held the command and levied his own troops. It was soon after the accession of Gaius (A.D. 37), and probably at the time when Silanus was replaced by L. Piso (A.D. 38), that the change was made, for Dio Cassius (59. 20. 7) associates it with the name of the latter. No. 99 shows that even under the new state of things the Proconsul had troops at his disposal, for though L. Flaminius began his service before A.D. 38 he must have been killed at the end of the reign of Claudius or the beginning of that of Nero ; and the Saltus Philomusianus was not on the frontier, but probably belonged to the upland district N. of Simitthus of which the Saltus Burunitanus formed part (*C. I. L.* viii. 10570. Bruns, *Fontes,* p. 258). In the second century we know that a cohort was still detached from the legion for this service (*C. I. L.* viii. 2532 Ab, speech of Hadrian at Lambaesis: *cohors abest quod omnibus annis per vices in officium pr[ocons]ulis mittitur*).

The Imperial legatus who was put in command of the legion was, like the legati of the two Germanies (see p. 108), originally entrusted only with the defence of a military frontier. He differed from them, however, in being inferior in rank (a *praetorius*) to the governor in whose province he was stationed, and in not having, at least before the end of the second century, an independent territorial sphere of action (Dio Cassius, 59. 20. 7, writes from the point of view of later times : δίχα τὸ ἔθνος νείμας ἑτέρῳ τό τε στρατιωτικὸν καὶ τοὺς νομάδας τοὺς περὶ αὐτὸ προσέταξεν). His proper title was *legatus Augusti pro praetore provinciae Africae* (*C. I. L.* viii. 2747), or *legatus pro praetore exercitus Africae* (*C. I. L.* v. 531. Cf. Tac. *Hist.* 4. 49: *tum legionem in Africa regebat Valerius Festus*). Hence we find him regularly engaged in public works in the Pro-

consular province (*C. I. L.* viii. 10048, road from Carthage to
Theveste, made in A.D. 123 *per leg(ionem) III Aug(ustam).
P. Metilio Secundo leg. Aug. pr. pr.* Contrast with this the
conflict of authorities in Germany and Gaul. Tac. *Ann.* 13.
53, esp. 4 : *invidit operi Aelius Gracilis Belgicae legatus deter-
rendo Veterem ne legiones alienae provinciae inferret*). It is
not till the third century that his title becomes *legatus Augusti pro praetore provinciae Numidiae* (*C. I. L.* viii. 2392).

> Mommsen, *Ephemeris Epigraphica*, iv. p. 537.
> Cagnat, *L'Armée Romaine d'Afrique*, 30.

The Roman Army in Egypt.

100.

C. I. L. iii. *Suppl.* 6809. On the pedestal of a statue erected by the city of
Alexandria to the commander of the Roman army in Egypt at his native town,
the colony of Antioch in Pisidia (it belonged to the Sergian tribe, cf. l. 2) on
the site of which the inscription was found. l. 5: *p(rimo)p(ilo)*. l. 16:
h(onoris) c(ausa).

```
        P · A N I C I O
        P · F · S · M A X I
        MO · PRAEFECTo
        CN DOMITI AENoBAR
   5    BI · P · P · LEG XII · FVLM PRÆF
        CASTROR · LEG II · AVG · IN
        BRITANNIA · PRAEF EXER
        CITV · QVI · EST · IN · AEGYPTo
        DONATO · AB · IMP · DONIS
  10    MILITARIBVS · OB EXPEDI
        TIONEM · HONORATo
        CORONA · MVRALI · ET
        HASTA · PVRA · OB BELLVl
        BRITANNIC · CIVITAS
  15    ALEXANDR · QVAE · EST
        IN · AEGYPTO · H · C ·
```

K 2

Under Augustus the garrison of Egypt consisted of three legions (Strabo, 17. 1. 12, p. 797: ἔστι δὲ καὶ στρατιωτικοῦ τρία τάγματα, ὧν τὸ ἓν κατὰ τὴν πόλιν ἵδρυται, τἄλλα δ' ἐν τῇ χώρᾳ, thinking probably of the state of things at the time of his own visit to Egypt in B.C. 24. Mommsen, *Eph. Epigr.* v. p. 9). By the time of Tiberius it was reduced to two (Tac. *Ann.* 4. 5. 4), which were united in a single camp at Alexandria (Josephus, *B. J.* 2. 19. 8: τὰ κατὰ τὴν πόλιν Ῥωμαίων δύο τάγματα). The principle of excluding Senators from the government of Egypt was extended to the command of these legions, which, as we learn from No. 100, was held not by one of the regular (senatorial) *legati*, but by an officer of purely military origin called *praefectus exercitus qui est in Aegypto*, who can be none other than the *praefectus castrorum*, who would naturally be in charge of the double camp at Alexandria (Josephus, *B. J.* 6. 4. 3: στρατοπεδάρχης τῶν ἐπ' Ἀλεξανδρείας δύο ταγμάτων. Cf. Tac. *Ann.* 1. 20. Wilmanns, *Eph. Epigr.* i. p. 91).

It appears from ll. 3–5 that Cn. Domitius Ahenobarbus (died A.D. 40, Suet. *Nero*, 6) the father of the Emperor Nero, was elected *duumvir* at Antioch, and, as was the case when persons of distinction (generally members of the Imperial family) accepted municipal magistracies, appointed as his deputy (*praefectus*) P. Anicius Maximus. Maximus began his military career in Syria (for the Twelfth Legion in Syria, cf. Tac. *Ann.* 15. 6. 5, 26. 1. Mommsen, *Res Gest. D. Aug.* 68, note 2), and it will be to this time that the expedition mentioned in l. 10 belongs. After attaining the rank of first centurion of the legion (l. 5), he was sent to Britain in the invasion of A.D. 43 with the Second Legion as *praefectus castrorum*, and earned the rewards stated in ll. 11–14. He was then promoted to the command of the Roman troops in Egypt, and while there received this mark of distinction from the city of Alexandria, probably towards the end of the reign of Claudius or under Nero.

GENERAL INDEX.

––•••––

[Numbers in ordinary type refer to pages; in thick type to the inscriptions. The number following a full stop after an inscription number indicates the line of the inscription, e. g. **38.** 7. The most important reference in each case is given first.]

A.

ACTA PRINCIPUM, iusiurandum in, 86, 72.
  fratrum Arvalium, **66,** 53, 84.
AERARIUM, administration of the, 104, 105.
  share of the, in providing corn for Rome, 31.
  maintenance of Imperial roads by the, 35.
  maintenance of aqueducts at Rome by the, 89.
AFRICA, Roman military arrangements in, 128-130.
  Imperial legatus in, 129-131, 77.
  protected native communities in, 15, 39.
AGRIPPA, M. VIPSANIUS, aqueducts of, at Rome, 29, 88, 89.
  recognised by Gaius as his ancestor, 71.
AGRIPPINA, the elder, married to Germanicus, 43.
  funeral honours paid to, by Gaius, **54, 71.**
AGRIPPINA, the younger, mother of Nero, 43.
  AUGUSTA, 42.
  makes Burrus praefectus praetorio, 74.
ALPS, conquest of the, 37.
  political organisation of the, 38-40, 101, **90.**
AMICUS CAESARIS, 103.
ANAUNI, citizenship of the, ratified by Claudius, 101-103, **91.**

ANDARTA, Celtic divinity, 14.
ANNONA, see ROME.
ANTIOCH in Pisidia, 23, 131, 132.
ANTONIUS, Eastern Empire of, 2, 21.
  rehabilitation of, by Gaius, 72.
AQUEDUCTS, at Rome, of Augustus, 28.
  at Rome, of Claudius, 88.
  administration of the, 29, 89.
ARA ROMAE ET AUGUSTI:
  at Lugudunum, **16, 17,** 48.
  at Narbo, 49.
  at Tarraco, 49, 10.
  Ubiorum, 49, 108.
  Liburniae, 49.
ARA AUGUSTI at Narbo, 53.
  NUMINIS AUGUSTI at Forum Clodii, 58.
  FORTUNAE REDUCIS, **38.** 7, 53.
  PACIS AUGUSTAE, **38.** 11, 53.
ARCA GALLIARUM, **36,** 51.
ARCITECTUS ARMAMENTARII IMPERATORIS, 77.
ARMENIA, Roman relations with, under Augustus, 22.
  occupation of, under Nero, 126, 119.
ARMY, of Africa, 128-130.
  of Dalmatia, 113.
  of Egypt, 132.
  of Germany, **14,** 75, 79, 81, 108.
  of Moesia, 117, 119, 120.
  of Pannonia, 19.
  of Spain, 10.
  of Syria, 126.
ASIA, province of, Commune, 48.

INDEX OF NAMES.

———◆◆———

COGNOMINA.

[Only the most important are given.]

GEOGRAPHICAL INDEX.

———•+———

[Only names which occur in the inscriptions are given — References to the
numbers unless otherwise stated.]

THE END.